When Enlightening Strikes

Creating a Mindset

For Uncommon Success

Stephanie Staples

Rave Reviews for *When Enlightening Strikes*

"When Enlightening Strikes is a captivating book about how to turn everyday experiences into powerful life lessons. It will catapult you forward to creating your true self."

Kathy B. Dempsey, author of *Shed or You're Dead®: 31 unConventional Strategies for Growth & Change*

"I love this book! Stephanie has opened up her heart and poured it on paper and you can't help but be enlightened after reading her delightful stories. You will learn that you can be and do more than you ever thought possible. Stephanie shows you how to put thoughts into action and live a happier life."

Lea Brovedani, author of *Trusted: A Leader's Lesson*

"Stephanie is a woman who doesn't just walk her talk, but invites us to take her hand and join her on the journey. Her candid story is sprinkled with humor, teachable moments and personal revelations, making her book an entertaining read that is truly enlightening."

Debbie Pokornik, author of *Break Free of Parenting Pressures, Embrace Your Natural Guidance*

"When Enlightening Strikes is a timely jolt of humor and hope that will inspire you to live a bigger life. Life lessons are everywhere if we just open our eyes; this book shows you where to look."

Michelle Cederberg, author of *Energy Now*

"Stephanie Staples has created a book that balances wonderful writing and laugh-out-loud humor with excellent insights into human psychosocial growth and behavior. Readers will not only be entertained by Stephanie's stories, they will be invited to examine their own 'enlightening strikes,' while learning concrete, useable strategies for happier lives."

Dr. Laura Sokal, Ph.D.

"So many times I laughed out loud, and I never do that with books. I cried out loud, too, and I never do that with books. I realized that I can be a better person after reading this book."

Susan Sweeney, eight-time best-selling author

When Enlightening Strikes

Creating a Mindset

For Uncommon Success

Stephanie Staples

When Enlightening Strikes: Creating a Mindset for Uncommon Success

Published by Your Life, Unlimited

Cover design by Yvonne Parks

Edited by John Hindle

Illustrations by John B. Junson

Author photograph by Ruth Bonneville

Printed in Canada

ISBN 978-0-9739432-1-4

Self-help, personal growth, psychology, inspirational

Disclaimer: The purpose of this book is to educate and entertain. It is a true story and the characters and events are real. In some cases, the names, descriptions and locations have been changed, condensed or combined for storytelling purposes but the overall chronology is an accurate depiction of the author's memory of the experience. Tips in this book are intended as a general guidance only and are not specific to any individual reader. Readers are encouraged to seek professional advice and neither the author nor publisher shall be liable or responsible for any loss or damage arising, or alleged to arise from, (directly or indirectly) any information or suggestions in this book.

For information on special sales or bulk purchases call: 204-255-5912

This book is dedicated

to you, because you know that

there is something more out there and you

are ready and willing to go find it!

Enlightening Strikes

Part Three – Your Life, Unlimited

Introduction

"Aha moments" don't work. This popular concept has been embraced by many and signifies a sudden insight. A good thing to be sure, it will elicit a head nod or an "oh, yeah," but that's generally it — and that's not enough. Why? Because shortly after the "aha moment" we usually go right back to doing the same old things in the same old way we did before the "aha." We might *think* differently for a while, we may even *feel* differently for a short space of time, but generally, we don't *act* different for a sustained period of time.

That's where "Enlightening Strikes" comes in and beats out the "aha moment" every time! They are those moments that can change everything. They are powerful enough to not only give you new insight into a situation, but they also leave you empowered to take immediate action to make positive change happen. You see, the insight is only half the equation — it's what you do after the insight that really matters. Think, feel, act. The action you take after the strike of enlightening is what changes your world for the better. That is what leads to uncommon success, a type of success that can seem so elusive in our chaotic world. Uncommon success is not defined by your bank account, your accomplishments, your status or your "stuff;" uncommon success is defined by your feelings.

The problem is that so many of us are so caught up just getting through the day, that we are missing out on the magic that is our life. We may be so busy *doing*, that we forget to check in every once in a while and ask ourselves how we are *feeling*.

So, I'm asking: How are you feeling?

Do you feel happy, satisfied, empowered?

Do you feel that there are ideas, insights and inspiration everywhere?

Do you feel that you live in a world where opportunities and possibilities abound and every question has an answer, even if it's not quite the answer you wanted to hear?

Do you feel pleased with your relationships, your livelihood, with yourself?

To be able to answer "yes" to these questions, at least the *majority* of the time, that is uncommon success. That could be you!

To get there, we must learn to shift our mindset from lack, pessimism and negativity to abundance, optimism and gratitude — this is what will open the door for uncommon success. To learn to *sustain* the uncommon success for the long term we must constantly be recharging our minds with the right type of energy and executing the actions to keep the momentum going. Extreme happiness in all areas of your life

12

awaits and it's not just for *other* people; it's not just for the privileged few; it is for you and me. And why not? We deserve it, too!

When Enlightening Strikes — Creating the Mindset for Uncommon Success is about real life, with all of its ups and downs, problems and delights. It's about those situations in our lives that leave an indelible imprint on us, for better or for worse. It is about learning to recognize in those moments, some profound, and some seemingly insignificant, the opportunity to grow, evolve and progress to the next level.

In the pages of this book, you will read about how one simple, but life-changing decision altered everything in my world for the better. Slowly, but surely, that decision has positively influenced every aspect of my life. As I lay out some of the challenges, follies, and moments that have shaped and impacted me, you will get a glimpse of a personal "rebranding" of sorts — a reinvention, an evolution of self. I was not a positive person by nature, not inherently self-motivated, nor a born leader — so I had to find ways to allow these qualities into my life. I soon realized that nothing in my world was going to change until I changed. Years later, I continue to grow, evolve and change.

A realistic life-goal is not to be perfect, but to acknowledge and appreciate who we are and where we are right now, and to recognize that there is always the prospect of something more, should we decide to go find it.

A realistic life-goal is not to be problem-free, but to be able to coach ourselves to move from setback to solution quickly and take the wisdom learned to make the next situation better. To turn obstacles into opportunities and to create a mindset that is so focused on personal growth that rarely a day goes by without a sign, an idea or a tool to help us keep on developing would be amazing.

This book was written to help you reach your own personal best, to see that it is not just about finding out the person you *are*; it's about doing what you need to do to create who you want to *be*. It is not just the big, important decisions you make that sculpt your life or your character; equally important are the small, seemingly inconsequential choices you make every day. Those small, consistent, proactive choices will be what craft your strong, positive, dynamic future.

My wish for you is that you journey *with* me as the stories unfold, and that you connect the dots from my life to yours, finding your own personal inspiration along the way.

Whether you read this book alone, with a partner or as part of a group of like-minded people, think of me as your virtual coaching partner, whose mission it is to help you become more resilient, more productive, more insightful and more fulfilled. Having other people on board is a great way to create support for your personal best quest — you will have lots of fodder for discussion! Try the ideas that resonate with you; challenge yourself to try the ideas you don't like, or combine, twist and turn the ideas to make them your own before incorporating them into your world.

In the end, it's your book, your life, your decision. So, rather than giving advice, I extend a warm invitation to you, an invitation to get to know yourself better. This book is an invitation to look at things from a new and more positive perspective, an invitation to find uncommon success for yourself, now! After all, if not now, when?

Thanks for joining me. Let's take this journey to create a mindset for uncommon success together, because amazing things happen when **enlightening** strikes.

Part One – Confessions of a Motivational Speaker

Happiness Check

"I am myself for a living." James Taylor

Hello, my name is Stephanie and I am a motivational speaker. I have just "come out."

Whew, that feels excellent! I am free to be me! In the past, I would never have uttered those words out loud let alone put them on paper for others to see. In my line of work calling yourself a motivational speaker is taboo, speaker suicide, a career killer.

You see, when I started out in this business my colleagues all gave me the same advice: Whatever you do, *don't* call yourself a motivational speaker — the audiences will chew you up and spit you out. People might have preconceived notions about motivational speakers; people might not take you seriously, and people might not…and on and on it went.

It was a firm warning, and I thought they knew best, so I listened to them. At all costs, I told myself, I will *not* call myself a motivational speaker.

And so I would let the meeting planners name me whatever they wanted. I spoke everywhere from tiny church basements, to the world-renowned Mayo Clinic, and most every place in between. Sometimes they called me an "expert in personal growth and development," or a "life enrichment coach," or my personal favorites, a "life/balance" or "stress management" speaker. Though what I do encompasses all those things; I had never uttered those words in any of my presentations.

While my main niche has been speaking with nurses, I will happily speak to anyone with a life. So bring on the construction worker conventions, engineer symposiums; you name the group, I've likely spoken to them.

While flowers, applause and standing ovations are great, I feel that it is an honor and a privilege to share my message and ideas with an audience. Every time I speak, I hope that something I talk about will resonate with them, and have a positive impact on their lives. In return, they give me the gift of engagement. No matter the size of the room, I can feel when the mood shifts and the energy lifts. I can sense when people begin to feel more hopeful, empowered and alive, like they have been inspired; they have been…motivated! Uh oh, I better be careful; I certainly don't want to be labeled a motivational speaker!

After the presentations, however, long after the crowd is gone, I sit alone and read the evaluations. I am not sure what other career gets evaluated quite as much. It's a weird thing, strangers judging you like that, writing whatever they want with no names or strings attached.

Not everyone is ready to hear my message. While the great majority of the audience may appreciate that I am a "fireball of positive energy," there is always that one evaluation that sticks out like a sore thumb. The one I remember most said: "You are lost and hopeless." Ouch. Oh, and there is always someone who doesn't like my hair or what I am wearing and feels the need to tell me so. My head knows that you can't please everyone, but my heart wonders why it's the negative messages that we remember the most.

The greater percentage of the participants, however, are kind and want to be inspired, happy and motivated. They want to believe in their own potential and they need other people to believe in them, even if it's a complete stranger. Life can be hard, sad, complicated and overwhelming. Most people *want* to know how to find and maintain the time, energy and motivation to live life better. Some people are happy being miserable. That's okay, that's where they are, and I know that I have to leave them there for now. I can tell by reading the comments that I usually strike a home-run with most people, that what I say and do has an impact, that I can and do make a difference. Most of the time it is clear that the message that was in my head and in my heart was expressed in such a way to make an impression on theirs. I love my work!

The most frequent comment I hear from people is, "I never thought of it that way." This is a wonderful thing to hear, because part of my job is to make people think. I am with them for a short amount of time, so my goal is to leave them with a message that lingers, that keeps them thinking about life in a new way.

My wonderful audiences also write things on their evaluations that lead me to believe I must indeed be perfect: "You must never get angry." "I wish you lived at my house." "You are the most positive person I have ever met."

Really?

I have to chuckle. Of course I'm positive, that's my *job*! In a way, I get paid to be happy. After all, who wants a negative, cranky motivational speaker? I have to be careful though, or I might fall into that trap and start to believe everything they write about me. I might begin to think I really *am* that great. Luckily for me, my wonderful family constantly reminds me that I am no more special or enlightened than anyone else, and am as normally abnormal as the next gal. I show my family these evaluations and they have a hearty laugh!

Speaking of laughing, I am considered to be a humorous speaker. "Hilarious!" they write, "A stand-up comedienne with a message." Yet, when I ask my kids if they think I'm funny, they tell me that I'm embarrassing…and to stop talking to their friends. When I ask my husband if he thinks I'm funny, "not really," is his honest answer. Sensing my disappointment, he adds, "Maybe we are just *used* to you."

When I thought about what I wanted to be when I grew up, what I am doing now would have been nowhere on the radar. Weren't motivational speakers people who had scaled mountains, paddled around the world, lost a few limbs or done something that makes your jaw drop open? I haven't done any of those things; in fact, I'm pretty boring.

Yep, this motivational speaker is pretty much the polar opposite of what you may imagine. I wonder if people would think less of me if they knew my *real* story.

It Sucks To Be Plain

"Plain: average, ordinary, simple, lacking beauty or distinction." yourdictionary.com

Yep, that pretty much sums up how I feel about my school-age self. Ask my teachers. They won't remember me. I am exceedingly average — not especially good, not exceptionally bad. Not too much to remember.

I am the last of four children raised by first generation Canadians, both descendents of Italian parents. In my eyes, my siblings had everything I did not. My sister Lorraine, 13 years my senior, was brilliant and knew *everything*; I was certain. My eldest brother, Paul, was gorgeous, as handsome as they get and adored by all. Closest in age, at eight years older was Vic, a talented musician, a self-taught guitarist who was on the road to rock stardom. They had it all. It was painfully clear to me that all of my parents' good genetic material had gone to them, with nothing left for me. And so my mindset was established at a very young age — poor me.

Some might say I was a surprise, but my lovely mother maintains to this day I was a blessing, delivered in her 40th year. I love my mother — my greatest fan. But, having raised three other gregarious, children, Mom was tired. She had neither the energy, nor the inclination, to chase me down. She says she always felt "grandmother-ish" compared to the other mothers, but I didn't notice that; I knew I was

22

loved. Mom worked hard, stuck in that in-between generation that both took care of everything at home *and* held down a full-time job, with nary a speck of help from my father. His involvement with his children was minimal at best. As was expected of the men of his day, he was a good provider.

I have just a few memories of my Dad and me together. The nights we would make banana splits complete with a special dish and adorned with all the fancy toppings we could find, like chocolate sauce, coconut, cherries, nuts, whipped cream....mmmm. Of course, we had all this right before bed, so I can conveniently blame all my bad eating habits on Dad. (Over) eating would be the only thing we would have in common for two decades, until my first child was born.

One of the best things my Dad ever did for me was on my 16th birthday. As a surprise, he'd taken the morning off work to take me to get my driver's license. Secretly, he'd had an extra key for his car cut, put it on a keychain and wrapped it up — all by himself. This may have been the only gift he ever thought of, bought and wrapped in his entire life. I discovered a side to my Dad I had not known before. He was a hero to me that day. Surprises were my new favorite thing.

It strikes me as funny how Mom could buy every other gift, make every other occasion special, but this is the only gift I remember. Sometimes being a Mom is a thankless job.

23

Educate This!

"Education is an admirable thing, but it is well to remember from time to time that nothing that is worth knowing can be taught." Oscar Wilde

There are two places in school that the truth comes out. The first is in report cards, and mine were not good. If you saw them you would find a sea of C minuses and D's, with just one lonely A — in typing, wow. The comment sections would be more revealing still: achievements below capabilities, little effort this term, disruptive behavior, poor use of class time, more home study required, assignments incomplete, vocational classes recommended. And so it was etched in stone that, clearly, I was not smart.

The second place the truth comes out at school is in gym class. Maybe you too remember the dreaded "picking of teams." I should like to meet the yahoo that decided this ridiculous practice was *actually* a good idea. While the incident itself lasts only moments, the effects of its impact can last an entire lifetime. I hope this practice has been abandoned in favor of something less emotionally scarring.

My classmate Andy and I usually alternated being picked last; we would give each other a sympathetic smile as we slugged out to the baseball diamond with our respective teams. You knew you were not welcome on this team, because they wanted to win, and you were not going to help them accomplish their goal. They had a system, a plan that didn't include you, since everyone knew what your contribution would be. With you as their handicap, they would aim for damage control, at best.

When it was my turn at bat I wanted more than anything to hit that ball over their heads and out of the park. I wanted to prove them wrong for choosing me last. I picked up the bat — it felt foreign in my hand. I took my practice swing; I imagined the ball making a wonderful arc in the blue sky, the kids chasing it as I made my way past base, after base, after base. Ready to take my swing, I looked up to give the pitcher the nod that I was ready. Then I saw them. Every one of the outfielders were moving to the infield to await my pathetic little tap of the ball. I felt everything inside (that hadn't already been stamped on), sink. I wanted so much to prove them wrong. I uttered a silent prayer for strength that I didn't have, to travel through the bat and flow into the ball. I swung, and predictably, I tapped the ball as was expected of me, not even getting to first base. They expected little of me, and that is exactly what they got. It seems low expectations garner equally low results. Funny how that works.

And so that sums up my school years — neither an athlete nor an academic. I didn't know where I fit in or who I was supposed to be. But I did know that I was, in a word, forgettable.

That's my pity-party and I'll cry if I want to.

Home Is Where the Hurt Is

"History keeps her secrets longer than most of us. But she has one secret that I will reveal to you tonight in the greatest confidence. Sometimes there are no winners at all."
John le Carré

I knew I could tell no one; no one else would understand.

I had a hate that was so deep; it felt like it was eating my soul. This hate was not for someone who wronged me, not for someone who abused me; it was for someone who loved me. It was my shame. If people knew about it, they would surely hate me too.

She was a roly-poly, white-haired lady in her seventies, who laughed easily and chatted in her thick Italian accent with anyone who would listen. Her pleasant smile and jovial personality were her calling card. She was my maternal grandmother. In an ironic twist of fate, I was named after her. I wanted to change my name to Kate. Everyone called her Nonna, everyone but me. I wouldn't call her anything.

When I was in my early teens, she came to live with our family. My siblings had long since spread their wings and flown the coop so it was just Mom, Dad, me and now, Nonna. I don't remember exactly when I started hating her but it took root, went deep and held tight and long.

Mom and Dad had a challenging relationship - unhappy, it seemed to me. I am sure they loved each other in their own way, but it was difficult to tell. I often wondered why they didn't divorce; marriage it appeared was an awful thing. If this is how it went, who on earth would want to be married? Add Nonna to the mix and it spelled disaster. Dad and Nonna were at odds constantly. There was so much yelling, so much unhappiness. Mom was always in the middle trying to make peace and I was adding to the grief.

Our family was in turmoil; that I knew, but what I didn't realize at that young age was that we badly needed help. *I* badly needed help. But no one offered and of course, we didn't ask. Every day was a catastrophe waiting to happen. Blood was boiling; everyone was on edge; no one was happy. This was my normal and it was not fun.

I desperately wanted to get out of the house; adulthood could not come fast enough for this chick. I knew a *good* person wouldn't hate like this, but it was the only tool I had. I channeled my hatred for the situation in my house to my grandmother, because I could. It was all I knew how to do.

It was only later that I could see my poor mother was stuck in the middle. She was trying desperately to keep her daughter, husband and mother happy — sacrificing her own sanity to do so. She couldn't be on everyone's side. She was in the middle of a war that would never be won.

27

As I was nearing the end of high school and it was time to pick a career, I chose nursing. Nurses were nice people who cared about others. They helped, they didn't hate. I thought maybe, if I became a nurse, that the hating, and the hurting, would stop.

Life can be a messy business. It seems that sometimes the love, the pain and the beauty can get all jumbled up together. Good or bad, circumstances can define you forever, if you let them. This one defined me as "bad."

I wonder if everyone has a secret.

And So He Came to Pass

"Character building begins in infancy and continues until death." Eleanor Roosevelt

I became a nurse and moved out of the house. Despite my uncertainties of marriage in general, I found Randy, a man I couldn't resist and took the plunge at the tender age of 22. He was wonderful and kind; he knew me and loved me unconditionally. We started a family and life was fine. I was neither especially happy nor exceptionally unhappy, neither excited about life nor disenchanted. I went through the motions, as was expected. No matter how good things were, something always felt a bit off. I was content, but I wanted something more. What that "something more" was, I did not know. Then there was the guilt for having those feelings. Why wasn't I as happy as I should be?

Everyone has something that rocks his or her world; mine was my father's death. I was eight months pregnant with my second child when Dad had his final heart attack. It did not take him instantly. Instead, he remained in the intensive care unit, connected to the machines that delivered the life-preserving medicine that kept his heart beating.

It seemed like seconds, and also years, passed as we waited for the medical team to debate his fate. The gavel fell on June 24. Dad was not going to get better and could not go on living like this. Although my father could not speak during

29

this ordeal, he was completely aware of what was going on. The doctors explained to all of the family, and to him, what was about to transpire. We would gather in a small room together, the drip that contained his life-supporting medicine would be stopped, he would close his eyes and would be gone within a few moments. He nodded his head in agreement. Can you imagine what would be going through your head if you knew you only had a few hours left on this earth?

We knew exactly what was going on in my Dad's head, because he motioned for pen and paper. We anxiously waited to see what poignant message he would write. Would it be an "I love you," a thank you note, an apology? Would it be words of wisdom or some final advice? Nope, instead he wrote a note with these words: "Bring my pension check for me to sign."

That was my Dad. I recall at the time being very upset with that note. Who on earth cares about your damned check, I had thought. What are you thinking?

Now I see that, in his way, he was thinking about his wife of 40 years, and what he could do to make things easier for her when he was gone. Maybe that's why he built the garage and bought a new car — to make her life easer. Maybe he had known that he would not see his 70th year. I guess it had been an "I love you" note after all.

Dad showed courage and bravery up until his last breath. It was the most amazing thing I had ever witnessed. With all the family gathered around, he moved peacefully out of our world, but not before he shooed my brother away from blocking the fan that was keeping him cool.

The funny thing is that stoicism, bravery and courage were not characteristics that I would have attributed to Dad during the previous 25 years. I could see that he had dug deep to pull out what characteristics he had needed to help himself and his family during the toughest of times. Character building really can continue until death; I saw it happen with my own eyes.

At his funeral, I listened while people said kind words about him and I couldn't help but wonder if *he* had ever heard people say those things *to* him when he was alive. How often do we think something nice about someone but not share that information with the person? What are we afraid of? Rejection? Embarrassment? Why hadn't I said something nice to him?

As I sat in the chapel, I couldn't help but think about what the proverbial "they" would say about me at my funeral, and then I thought about what I would *want* them to say about me.

And that is when I had the first and most profound

Enlightening strike. I didn't know what it was at first. It was foreign, new, strange. It seemed to speak as loud and as real as the voices I was hearing in the chapel. Its message? That what I would *want* people to say about me when I was gone and what they *would* likely say about me were two totally different things. Yikes, talk about a wakeup call! For a moment it welled up in me. And then: KAPOW! Along came another realization: I was not dead yet! I had complete and total power over this situation! If my Dad could reinvent himself on his deathbed, then surely I could too — especially since I was young, healthy and willing to make a conscious and concerted effort. The barbell of life had been lifted from my shoulders, the shift was immediate and suddenly, I was eager to begin anew!

I made a life-changing decision that day. I decided that if I did not like the "me" that I was, that I could and would create a "me" that I could get excited about — someone who I wanted to spend the rest of my life with, someone who would leave a positive legacy for her children and her community, someone who would make her husband proud and someone who, at the end of her days, would have made the world a better place. For the first time in my life I thought not about who I *was,* but about who I could *become.*

I chose not to be limited by the labels impressed upon me as a child, labels that were cast by others, or labels that I assumed. If the beliefs didn't suit the person I wanted to become, then I would no longer accept them.

Old stories be damned! I do enough; I have enough and I am enough. I decided to affirm myself, and keep reaffirming myself, until I made it my truth. I would no longer be among the huge percentage of the population that has low self-esteem. I would commit one per cent of my day to personal development. That's only about 14 minutes; I could do that.

I decided to read books from the minds of the brilliant, to listen to audios that would reshape my thinking. I decided to turn my commute time into "college in the car" by listening to the masters teach. I went to every personal development seminar I could afford, and some that I couldn't. I was a sponge, soaking up what I liked and leaving the rest (because sometimes I was not ready to hear that message yet). I sought out engaging people and mentors, asked many, many questions and let the answers steep.

I decided to be among the top three per cent of the population that care enough to use their time, energy and money to better themselves. I knew that I might fall off the bandwagon many times over the years, succumbing to those old stories, but vowed to climb back on board every time. That is what really matters, after all — picking ourselves up after we fall down.

I know now that who we are at any age is a mere snippet of who we are to become and that everything we do today is getting us ready for the next step. Who we are right now is a result of the thoughts and actions of yesterday. The true power resides in the thoughts, actions and feelings of *today*; that is what will define who we are tomorrow.

I had thought that the best gift Dad had given me was a key to his car, but on the day of his death he gave me a far greater gift — he gave me my new life. In that moment I dedicated my future to my own personal growth, to working harder on myself than on anything else. This was the first in a series of events and choices that taught me how to create a mindset for uncommon success and how to coach myself happy. Who knew that the decision I made that day would affect thousands of others?

P.S. One month to the day after Dad died, my lovely Kara was born, and for a few days, she looked just like him!

WORK HARDER ON YOURSELF
THAN ANYTHING ELSE.

Part Two — The Reinvention Begins

It's Not a Matter of *If*, It's a Matter of *When*

"If I despised myself, it would be no compensation if everyone saluted me, and if I respect myself, it does not trouble me if others hold me lightly." Max Nordau

I knew it was not a matter of *if* I saw him again but *when*. The boy who broke my heart, crushed my dreams and dumped me right before high school graduation. His name was Dave, and I had loved him like only a 17-year-old could love.

It had been a humiliating breakup, the kind where one person is done and the other person is not. I, sadly, was the one who was not. I had begged and pleaded and embarrassed myself thoroughly. Ughh, it was pitiful. I wish I could rewind and leave with my head held high and self-respect intact. Have you ever had a totally mortifying breakup like that? Didn't you envision seeing that person again one day in the hope of regaining your dignity?

The next time I saw Dave, I was certain that not only would I *not* be pitiful, I would be strolling hand in hand with my gorgeous husband, who would be looking very satisfied and in love. Our three beautiful children would be perfectly clean, coiffed and well-behaved. Of course I would be looking radiant and fresh as a line-dried sheet (not that I've actually ever line-dried my sheets, but I imagine they are really fresh!). Well, that's not quite how it happened.

I innocently opened my backdoor to take out the garbage, and suddenly time stood still.

He was striding up the neighbor's sidewalk. I felt like I was in a movie and everything was going in slow motion. It was *him*, Dave, *my* Dave. But this was not the same young Dave I had last seen 10 years prior; this was a *man-Dave*. And a tall, dark and very handsome man he was too! He was wearing a striking uniform proudly proclaiming himself as one of our cities finest, and mmm…he *was* looking fine. The only thing missing was a horse.

On the other hand, I was having a few issues and was far from the "fair maiden" that used to date this prince.

Try to picture this scene: I was fresh out of the hospital from delivering my third baby. I had the garbage loaded in one hand and a newborn squirming in the other. I had dark circles under my eyes, spit up on my shoulder and Play-Doh stuck under my fingernails. It gets worse: shapeless, hand-me-down maternity clothes on, makeup off, needy, clawing toddlers hanging off each leg and oh, the crowning glory — my hair. Well, my hair with its grey roots showing was yanked back in a very messy, unflattering ponytail with "sexy" wisps dangling in my eyes. Argh! How was he supposed to feel bad about dumping *this?*

But here is the kicker, although I recognized him immediately, he had not noticed me. I ducked back into my house, lickety-split to avoid the potential crisis.

I had a very short time to make a very big decision. What would you have done? Stayed inside hiding and pretending that you never saw him? I was pretty sure I should hide and pretend like this never happened. In fact, every rational fiber in my body wanted to stay in the house, but somehow my legs won. They unlocked from their position of fear and they popped outside. I chose to call over to him. What *was* I thinking?

I boldly stepped out of the house. "Dave!" I said in an enthusiastic voice.

"Yes," he replied with a blank look in his eyes.

"Don't you know who I am?" I said, already crushed.

He looked me up and down for a moment, he lowered his eyebrows and cocked his head and then looked deep into my eyes. I saw the dots slowly connecting in his head. And finally, in a voice with an inflection I cannot adequately describe on paper, he said, "*Steph?*"

I nodded my head, sorry that my legs had won the fight. Couldn't we just rewind this story? I would like to review my decision. I'll take door number two: hide in the house, this time.

"*Ohhh, Steph*," he said in an almost pitiful tone. I wanted to curl up into a teeny tiny ball.

We made small talk and caught up on what had been happening. It was obvious to me that he had spent the last 10 years fighting crime and working out, and I am certain it was clear to him that I had spent the last 10 years making babies and *not* working out. It was a short conversation. I would have liked to go inside and walk barefoot over hot coals — that would have been less painful.

We politely wished each other well and went back to our respective lives. I suppose he did, anyway. On the other hand, I was completely devastated, crushed, mortified. I was mad at myself for even still caring about what he thought about me! I didn't want this guy back in my life, but was it wrong to want him to feel just a little bit bad for dumping me, to want to regain a little of my pride? I wanted to hide for another 10 years.

My wonderful Randy was upstairs and so I went up to spill the beans, "Guess who I just saw?"

"Who?"

"Dave."

"Dave? Old boyfriend Dave? Oh…did *he* see you?" He questioned.

"Yep," I replied.

In that same familiar, pitiful tone, my kind-hearted husband, who loved me no matter what, said, "*Ohhhh, Steph.*" Wow, you *know* you look bad when even your husband feels sorry for you in that situation!

I knew it was not a matter of *if* I saw Dave again, it was a matter of *when,* and the next time, I swore I'd be ready. Every day after that I got up, made-up, dressed up and did my hair up — just in case! I may have looked better on the surface, but something else needed to happen.

Bam-Enlightening Strikes

Sometimes *Enlightening* works through good-looking cops. That's okay; I'll take it however it comes!

Exercise, I needed to start exercising; I needed to feel good about myself emotionally *and* physically — from the inside out. And I needed to do it, not for Dave (he wasn't that great anyway), not for Randy (he loved me already), but for me.

With three little ones and a tight budget this will not be easy, but where there is a will, there is a way. I found a nearby gym that would let me work out as much as I wanted for free if I babysat for an hour a day. It's a deal.

Almost every day, I packed up my three little ones and off we'd go. Some days the last thing I wanted to do was bundle up three kids and lug them out into the cold. Some days the kids in the daycare were more than I could take, but most days I was very proud of myself for sticking to my commitment. That feeling was enough to overcome the tough part.

Ever so slowly, little by little, it began to work. I fell in love with exercising. Well, maybe love is too strong a word; I think I was more in love with the escape! It became my one hour out of the day that was just for me. After a while people started asking me if I had lost weight. I didn't know. I didn't own a scale. But my clothes *did* feel a little looser. I stepped on the gym scale, put the little weights where I thought they should be, and clunk, the bar went down. Hmm, I slid the weights farther down to the left, farther and farther. Finally, I got off the scale thinking it must be broken. I found another scale, hmmm! I *had* lost weight *and* I had more energy than ever before.

Since then, I have committed to making regular daily exercise a part of my life. I do it because I can, because I am well and healthy. I do it for others who can't. I do it in a spirit of gratitude to thank my body for getting me this far and to bribe it to get me further. I am committed to changing the exercises up so I don't get bored. I list all the things I can do to be active and I commit to doing one of those things when I want to and more importantly, when I don't. I promise to make time for what is important, and exercise is important, no excuses. I have committed to being active and vibrant and alive, everyday.

Maybe I should try baseball again? Nah.

What could you start doing today that would make you feel more alive?

YOU ONLY HAVE TO
EXERCISE TWO TIMES:
WHEN YOU WANT TO
AND WHEN YOU DON'T.

March It Out

"The word aerobics came about when the gym instructors got together and said, "If we're going to charge $10 an hour, we can't call it jumping up and down." Rita Rudner

Oh, how I loved going to that aerobic studio, I loved the classes, the music, the freedom...the adults!

I had my spot in the class. I always positioned myself in the back right-hand corner directly behind someone else (preferably someone larger than me), so that I couldn't see myself in those huge mirrors that lined the front of the studio. When the lady in front of me raised her arm, I raised my arm. When she raised her leg, I raised my leg. All I needed to see was her. Who wants to look at themselves in the mirror? Certainly not me. Those were the days of leotards and bodysuits. I was quite content in my T-shirt and sweats, thank you very much.

Things continued this way for many months. I was having fun and I was happy. Until one day when Maria, the gym owner, had a conversation with me that made my head spin. "Stephanie, how about moving from helping out in child care to teaching aerobics classes?"

Surely she must have been joking! I was the chubby one hiding in the back corner; I was the one picked last. Was I dreaming? Was she nuts? How on earth could I ever be the leader in front of the class *and* in front of the mirror! Clearly, she didn't know me very well.

I spat out an immediate "No thanks!" to her offer.

I shook my head for days trying to figure out why she had asked me to do this; it seemed so ludicrous. I asked my friends, "Isn't that the craziest thing you've ever heard, *me* teaching aerobics?"

"Why not?" was the general reply.

Why not? *Why not?* Only a million reasons.

Thump, **Enlightening** Strikes.

Maria believed in me. She was a smart lady. If *she* believed in me, perhaps I should work harder at believing in myself.

Have you ever had someone believe in you, more than *you* believe in you?

I began to reconsider. What if Maria wasn't nuts? What if I was passing up this opportunity? What if I *could* come to the front of the room? What if there was a leader in me somewhere and I just didn't know it yet?

This required a huge leap of faith. Have you ever stepped so far out of your comfort zone that you scared yourself silly? That is what I did; I scared myself silly. I signed up for the

Certified Fitness Leader class — me and a room full of 19-year-old university students.

I wish I could tell you that I was fabulous, but I wasn't. In fact, I was terrible! For what seemed like eternity I was a very bad instructor. Maybe you think I am exaggerating, that I wasn't really that bad; but I was! Just ask those poor, patient women who came to my first classes! I was off time, off beat, and off cue. I forgot my moves, patterns and order, and despite Maria's patient guidance, no, I couldn't "hear" the eight count — whatever that was.

Eventually though, I got the hang of the whole thing and even began to enjoy my own classes. I think the participants did too; at least they showed up when my name was on the schedule — that was a good sign! More importantly, looking back, I know that the ups and downs of this experience unequivocally paved the road for me to speak my truth to the masses today.

It all started with someone else believing in me and giving me the courage to trust, risk and try.

We all have the power to help someone else take flight. It requires time, energy and patience. You can empower others by telling them that you believe in them and by supporting them as they take flight. We might never know what our words, deeds or even our thoughts and prayers do for another.

Maybe the knowing doesn't matter as much as simply the doing.

You can choose to allow someone else's belief in you help you set big, wonderful, fulfilling goals.

And those mirrors...I know their purpose now. It's easy to see where someone else needs to improve, but it's not until we look at ourselves in the mirror that we can start improving ourselves.

IT'S MUCH EASIER
TO JUDGE OTHERS
BUT TO GROW, WE MUST
LOOK IN THE MIRROR.

The Worst Mother in the World

"I always wanted to be somebody. If I made it, it's half because I was game enough to take a lot of punishment along the way and half because there were a lot of people who cared enough to help me." Althea Gibson

Have you ever been tired? I mean really dragging your butt, barely functioning, tired? Well, that's how tired I was that day. I had just barely made it through my 7 a.m. to 3 p.m. shift at work and was trying to mentally prepare myself to take the baton from Randy, who was heading out the door for his evening shift. The exhaustion made me wonder how I would make it through the evening with the kids. I decided to take the easy way out. I got home, laid down on the floor and pretended I was mobile gym equipment. I let the kids climb all over me — they thought it was fun. Eventually though, they wanted to eat, and against my better judgement, I heard myself say words that made them very happy: "Who would like cookies for supper?" Surprise, everyone does and Mommy got to be the hero!

Bath time arrived, and just the thought of it exhausted me even further. It was a scorching August evening and I had a brilliant idea: "Everyone in your bathing suits and into the backyard!" I exclaimed, grabbing the hose. They thought it was a game, while I called it a shower. Good enough. Time for bed, *finally.*

As soon as I tucked my angels into bed, I had another bright idea. I decided to go lie down in the basement, where it was cooler. The heat and the humidity of the evening, the lack of air conditioning in our house and the fact that the heat had risen up to the second floor where the bedrooms were, led me to believe that this was, indeed, a good idea.

The kids never woke up during the night anymore and I was a light sleeper anyway. No worries — or so I thought. I hunkered down in the cool basement and immediately crashed.

The next thing I knew Randy was shaking me awake, "Stephanie! Stephanie!"

I remember feeling quite put off, "Not tonight. I'm sooo tired."

He persisted, "Stephanie, wake up!"

Didn't he know how tired I was? "Leave me be," I grumbled.

"Stephanie! Do you have any idea what has been going on in our house?"

Suddenly, I was wide awake. It was after midnight, and for me, the last three hours did not exist. Randy had to piece the story together for me.

Apparently, shortly after I went to sleep, our young son, Aaron, woke up and began to call for me, "Mommy, Mommy, where are you Mommy?"

48

I hadn't heard him, but his younger sister, Kara, had, so she joined in the searching and the shouting, "Mommy, Mommy, where are you Mommy?"

Again, I'd heard nothing, but their younger sister, Gina, did and she woke up and aided in the chorus.

They didn't know I was in the basement. And I had heard nothing.

The windows were all open and the neighbours had heard all of the screaming going on in our house, so eventually they decided that they had better do something. The fact that they took charge was a great blessing, even if we didn't know them. Elzbieta and Marik were new to our neighborhood, recent immigrants from Poland, whom we had met only briefly and who did not speak much English. Unsure what they would find when they came into our house they decided to come as a family, with their teenaged children. For good measure, and so as not to frighten our children, whom they barely knew, they also brought their beagle, Pinga!

For many hours, seven people and three dogs frolicked in our house. Our wonderful new neighbors pacified, played with and looked after my children, all the while, unbeknownst to them, I was comatose in the basement. They must have really wondered how parenting in Canada worked.

Imagine the shock when Randy came home from work at midnight to find a house full of near strangers, a new dog, his children dancing around, and his wife "missing."

Luckily, knowing me as he did, the first thing he asked was, "Did anyone look in the basement?" No one had.

After he told me what had been going on, I was devastated. How could I have let this happen? I felt like the worst mother in the world. It was a wonder that child and family services hadn't come to take my kids away. Can you envision the things that could have happened to those children in the hours I was "missing?" I couldn't even allow myself to go there.

I knew that I had been tired, but this was ridiculous. Something was definitely wrong and I needed to find out what. The next morning I went straight to the doctor's office and I am sure that no one was ever as happy as I was to be diagnosed with pneumonia. I was not the worst mother in the world, I was sick. Thank God!!

Then I did what anyone would do; I took my prescription, stopped by the florist and marched straight over to my neighbors to explain my case and extend my everlasting thanks and gratitude.

♪ **Enlightening** Strikes.

Sadly, sometimes enlightening strikes in the form of accident, illness, disease or devastation. Thankfully, it was gracious with me.

I did not just get pneumonia that day, or even that week. In retrospect, I had been tired, lethargic, overwhelmed and on my way to burnout for days, weeks, possibly months. But in my busyness, I had ignored the signs and symptoms. I had been wearing that special piece of apparel, maybe you have one — superwoman's cape. You see everyone depended on me. I had a job to do, people to care for, things to get done and if I slowed down, stopped, or even — heaven help us — got sick, well, surely the world would have fallen apart.

My world could have fallen apart that night, if my neighbors hadn't taken charge.

I swore that from that day forth I would pay attention to what my body was telling me, that I would take care of myself so that I could bring my best to the world. That day, I gave myself permission to take off my superwoman cape and value myself enough to make my own self-care a priority.

I vowed to listen to my body. I would never again let myself get so run down that I couldn't look after my own family. Whenever possible, I would go to bed when I was tired; I would ask for help and try not to be a one woman show. I would do something small for myself every day to validate this commitment. I would never again think that I am so self-important that the world could not function without me. I know now that I cannot give my best if I don't feel my best. I understand that self-care is not selfish; it is a gift I can give those I love.

YOU CAN'T DO GOOD
IF YOU DON'T FEEL GOOD
AND YOU WON'T FEEL GOOD
UNLESS YOU TAKE CARE
OF YOURSELF, FIRST.

Life's a Beach

"Most people spend more time and energy going around problems than in trying to solve them." Henry Ford

I was getting dizzy just watching this dog running back and forth in a frenzied search for something.

The early morning air was fresh, crisp and perfect and the beach was deserted, almost. A middle-aged woman was sitting in one of those old green mesh lawn chairs, engrossed in a paperback. It was just another gorgeous day at the beach, nothing out of the ordinary, except for that dog, which was not just an ordinary dog, but a dog in a state that I had never seen before. He was focused and intent. He was madly dashing back and forth along the white, sandy shoreline, and he was completely consumed. He ran about 50 feet to one side of his owner and then took a sharp hairpin turn to head 50 feet to the other side. Back and forth he went, again and again. It was a strangely hilarious sight. After watching this for a while, my curiosity finally got the best of me.

"Good morning. Do you mind if I ask what your dog is doing?"

"He's herding the waves," she said. "We come out here every morning and he does this."

Herding the waves? *Herding* the waves? Herding the *waves*? How odd.

"It's great," she continued, "I don't have to exercise him, we just come out here and he runs and I read."

"Hmmm, fascinating."

Dog lover that I am, I felt rather sorry for this poor old guy. Here he was at the beach, the beautiful, magnificent beach, and he was consumed with running around trying to control the waves that he would never, ever be able to get under control. It seemed to me he was unable to enjoy the beach, the water, his owner or anything else because he was all worked up trying to do something that was impossible.

Wait a minute. Running around trying to control everything, with no hope of ever getting everything under control? Hmm, that reminds me of someone. Wait a minute; that reminds me of just about everyone I know, including myself.

⚡ Oh my, is that an **Enlightening** strike near the water —
that could be dangerous!

Herding the waves, what a perfect metaphor for life! Life's a beach, after all. It is beautiful and it is here for us to enjoy but we are often so task oriented, so focused on getting things done, so busy trying to control things that we will never be able to control, that we often miss out on the beauty of the whole experience. Well, at least I do. What about you?

Our personal and professional responsibilities, tasks, jobs, and obligations are like those waves — things that we just *have* to do that keep pounding at us again and again. We work so hard to keep all our waves within our control that sometimes we drive ourselves and others crazy in the process. What if we take a time out, right here, right now, today? Whenever we get that feeling of excess stress coming on, when we start to feel that churning deep in the pit of our stomach, a sense of worry or lack of control, think about that old dog, think about waves. Think about all the external factors that we really have no direct power over and about what is within our circle of influence.

Know that what we focus on expands, so make a conscious effort to focus less on the problems and issues we have no control over. Let's put our time, thoughts and energy into focusing consistently and quickly on either acceptance or solutions. Whenever I forget, I think of the dog, the beach and the waves. I remind and re-remind myself that I should not and cannot control everything. But my thoughts, actions and feelings are waves that I *can* control, and that is a pretty powerful thing.

IF YOU DON'T LIKE THE WAY YOU ARE FEELING, CHANGE WHAT YOU ARE THINKING ABOUT AND YOUR FEELINGS WILL AUTOMATICALLY CHANGE, TOO.

This Hurts Me More Than It Hurts You

"Have the courage to face the truth. Do the right thing because it is right. These are the magic keys to living your life with integrity." W. Clement Stone

I'd blown it; I had made a mistake in my job. This was not just putting the wrong price on the wrong item; I was a nurse and I had just made a medication error. I had given the wrong medication to the wrong patient. Thankfully, it had been a non-narcotic painkiller and no harm was done, but still, I had made a medication error.

Distracted by needy patients everywhere, I was trying to deal with and help everyone. While preparing the lunchtime medications, I'd let the distractions take me away from my task. I'd crushed up one patient's pills, mixed them with applesauce and then let myself get sidetracked by someone else wanting my attention. I'd put the mixture down and dealt with the other issue. When I came back, I grabbed the crushed up pills and applesauce mixture and promptly put them in a completely different patient's mouth.

The second the lady swallowed the pills that weren't hers. It was too late to have her spit them out — the deed was done. Ugh. I knew I had a choice: report my error or carry on. It was just a pain pill after all; no one would be the wiser. But I knew I didn't really have a choice.

Eleanore was my superior. She had a strong presence, not formidable, but strong; she was a leader, fair and reasonable. I made my way down to her office and slunk in with my head hanging very low. I began to ramble… "I made a medication error. I gave this lady's meds to that lady because I got distracted and wasn't paying attention to what I was supposed to be doing. Next time, I will finish what I am doing and then move on to handle the next issue. I am so, so sorry." Eleanore just looked at me. I was panicky. And then she said words that I remember to this day: "When you make a mistake these are the four things we look for:

1) Accepting responsibility;

2) Remorse;

3) Reasoning to figure out why it happened;

4) A plan in place so that it does not happen again.

You have come into my office and you have addressed all of those things. Now go back to work."

Enlightening struck again. What complete and utter sense Eleanor's words made. I have since used these guidelines to address mistakes of all sorts, in all areas of my life. Those words she spoke all those years ago still resonate with me; they really define integrity.

We will not always be right or do right; but when we have integrity we step up; we accept responsibility for our actions.

58

We feel remorse and we have an understanding of why it happened so that we can put a plan in place to ensure it won't happen again.

While a bad reputation follows you around, living life with integrity actually precedes you. If we tell the truth even when we don't have to, do the right thing even when nobody is around to notice, consistently show up on time, do our best, keep our promises, etc., then people correctly assume we are persons with integrity. It becomes our character.

Integrity comes in very handy when we do make mistakes because people tend to give us the benefit of the doubt. Instead of saying, "Oh, she's always late," they might worry that we got into an accident because it happens so rarely.

If someone who doesn't know you well judges you harshly, the person who does know you might say, "She must be having a difficult day because she is not usually like that." If you make a mistake, it will be more easily forgiven. If we lack integrity, people will not trust, value or respect us. Having a high level of integrity is one of the most important characteristics we can possess. It is a core value; it is a choice, and it is something that we can nurture. Integrity is modeled all around us, yet its value in our society seems to be underrated. Integrity comes into play in everything we do. In fact it's more than everything we do — it's everything we are.

Coming from a place of integrity means being truthful and honest. It means being reliable, trying to build rather than break, help rather than hurt, connect rather than crumble. It means being authentic — being the same person whether people are watching or not. When I am wondering what the "right thing to do" is, I simply ask myself, what would a person with high integrity do? The answer then becomes crystal clear.

LEAD WITH INTEGRITY,
EVEN IF NO ONE IS LOOKING.

Make Room for a Crystal-Clear Yes!

"Saying no is the surest way to make more time in your life and it can have a deeper influence of empowering others."
Steph

Oh no, it's work calling.

"Hi, can you come for an evening shift tonight?" requests the tired, but pleasant voice on the other end of the line.

A hundred thoughts run through my head, reasons why I can't go into work, none of them true. I think about the time I said no because I couldn't get the car out in the snow storm, which *was* true. They sent a snowmobile to pick me up that night. Have you ever made an excuse for why you couldn't do something and then someone "solved" it for you? Yeah, that was great.

"Yes, I can come," I reply, angry that I don't have a good, honest reason for refusing the shift that night. I hang up the receiver a little too hard, then yell at the kids, yell at the husband, and yell at the dogs. I am mad, not at them, at myself. I did it again! Why can't I ever say no?

I know that the nurse on the other end of the line isn't trying to trap me or make me mad. She just needs to fill a shift; she just wants to go home herself. Still, why does it seem like everyone keeps putting things on my plate, do they think it's a platter? Steph can you help out on this committee; Honey, can you stop by the bank; Mom, can you get me that; Mrs. Staples, we were wondering if you wouldn't mind doing..., etc.

My response is always the same: Yes, sure, okay, you can count on me, I'd be delighted, is there anything else I can do?

Shoot me now!

Why does the word yes keep popping out of my mouth, when everything inside me is screaming nooooooo? I like people; I want to help people; I want people to like me. I know that my friends, colleagues and family are not (usually!) trying to make my life more difficult. I know that they are just thinking about their own needs, but all this "yes-ing" is driving me to an early grave. When will enough be enough?

ZAP — there it is again. **Enlightening,** ouch, what now?

Enough will be enough when, and only when, I say it is. Saying no more often will leave me with extra time and energy for additional, *enjoyable* things that I could say yes to. I need to get comfy with saying no. Very sensible, why didn't I think of that sooner?

I make a pact with myself — I promise to never say yes right away, unless it's a *crystal-clear* yes, a no-brainer, an "oh my God, I've been hoping you'd ask" sort of yes. Otherwise, I will pause and buy some time. I will tell them that I will get back to them in five minutes, five hours or five days, maybe even five months, depending on the request!

If someone must have an answer right away, I am prepared — "If you need to know right now the answer has to be no, but if you can give me some time to check things out, it's a definite maybe."

Saying no does not mean that I am selfish, unkind or lack compassion; it just means that it's not going to work out this time. I must ask myself: "Do I really want this? Do I really need this? Is this leading me closer to where I want to be, or further away?" If it doesn't fit, I can decline. If they don't like me because of it, I know that this is their issue. Could it really be that simple? Well, it is simple; it's just not always easy.

I've defined some rules for saying no. I try to be gracious and thank the individual for asking. If it's true, I'll say something like, "I would love to help you, but it is not going to work right now." Or "Please feel free to ask me again" (but only if I genuinely want them to ask again). I have stopped making a million excuses as to why I cannot accommodate their requests. I am polite, but I don't over-explain. In the past, my excuses were only serving to try to rationalize to *myself* why I was saying no; they rarely made a difference to the other person. Now, if I say no, I try very hard to ditch the unhealthy guilt that is often a part of it. I am saying no to the situation, not the person. I am choosing what is best for my life right now, not choosing to hurt them. I also use the power of negotiation. Sometimes it doesn't have to be a yes or no, it can be a win-win by creating a totally new deal. If I do, in my own time accept the request, I accept with a happy heart and not with a "you owe me, grrrr" feeling. If I choose it, I deal with it.

Cultivating a mindset to say no may take some courage, but a well said no makes room in my life for the things that are a crystal-clear yes!

SAYING NO TAKES
A BIT OF PRACTICE,
A BIT OF TACT
AND A LOT OF GUTS.

Take My Money, I Insist

"Sincerity is the key which will open the door through which you will see your separate parts, and you will see something quite new. You must go on trying to be sincere. Each day you put on a mask, and you must take it off little by little." G. I. Gurdjieff

Sometimes it's great to be a woman. Sometimes you just have to use it to your advantage. This was one of those times.

It was one of those bitterly cold Canadians nights when the wind chill drops the temperature to 40 below. Eager to escape the cold, I parked the car as close to the building as I could, wrapped my scarf around my head and hastily dashed into the building. An hour and a half later, I returned with a colleague, ready to head out for a nice steaming chai latté. When we got into my car, I turned the key and I heard the worst sound you can hear from a car in winter: nothing. Zip, zero, ziltch. I tried again, no response. I took a big breath, spoke ever so gently and sweetly to my car, adding a little begging and a prayer for good luck. I turned the ignition. Nothing. I realized in horror that I had left my lights on and the battery was dead — dead, dead, dead.

After the requisite head bang on the steering wheel and apology to my colleague, I ran back into the building with the hopes of using my "damsel in distress card" to find a Good Samaritan willing to brave the cold and give my car a boost.

At that exact moment, a well-dressed gentleman was leaving the building and offered me a helping hand. Color me happy!

The kind stranger boosted my dead battery with his truck quick as a wink, while my friend and I waited in the comparatively warm car. She suggested I give him a hug — it is Canada, after all — but instead I dug through my wallet looking for some cash. There was a five dollar bill and a twenty. A five didn't seem like enough, but a twenty seemed like too much. Well, I thought, as I grabbed the twenty, he won't take it anyway. I got out of my car and presented the big bill. "Thank you so much," I said.

"No problem," said Mr. Good Samaritan, waving off the money.

"Oh please, I really appreciate your help," I said, still holding out the money.

And then…he took it! He actually *took* my money. This is *Canada*, you are not supposed to actually *take* the money!

I was so shocked! Twenty bucks for a two minute boost? *Really*!

Well, there was no hug following that. My friend and I were both quite disgusted with the whole event. Somehow, having that "gentleman" accept my $20 had taken all of the niceness right out of the situation.

Hello, this is **Enlightening** calling. Is anyone home? What really happened here?

Rewind. I needed help; someone helped; I offered to pay him; he said no. I insisted; he accepted. So why was I so angry? I was upset simply because I had a pre-conceived notion that he should *not* accept my money. Clearly, he should want to boost my car out of the goodness of his heart!

As I stepped back from this situation and looked at it with a bird's-eye view, I saw that *I* was the one who was wrong. I had not been sincere in my offer. I was a phony. I never for a moment thought I would return to the car without my $20 bill. It absolutely served me right and taught me a lesson. I was the creator of that situation. If I had deemed that a heartfelt thank you would suffice, it would have. I chose to offer the money, therefore I had no right to judge him for taking it. I had been insincere.

As a result of this incident, I realized that I needed to reassess how sincerity showed itself in my world. In order to push my sincerity meter up a notch, I now try *not* to:

- Ask questions that I don't care to hear the answers to, or
- Offer things if I am hoping that the offer will be declined.

Instead, I try to:

- Think long and hard before I speak
- Deliver honest compliments
- Say what I mean in a tactful fashion
- Use well placed silence, instead of insincere words
- Ask myself if what is coming out of my mouth is in line with my true beliefs and values
- Notice the feelings that my body gives me when I am speaking sincerely

I want to feel calm, light and happy. I want uncommon success. When I am insincere, I feel agitated and am left with a feeling of dissonance; I feel stressed, heavy and unhappy. This is not the feeling of success.

Speaking my truth allows me to connect, on a deeper level, with both myself and with others. It's not always easy, but it always feels right.

And to Mr. Good Samaritan I say thank you for helping me, not only with my car, but with learning a truth about a very important value. And hey, have fun with the $20. I mean that, sincerely.

WHEN THE WORDS YOU SAY
MATCH THE VALUES YOU HAVE,
THE THOUGHTS YOU THINK
AND EMOTIONS YOU FEEL
— THAT'S SINCERITY.

Onemorethingitis

"Slow down and enjoy life. It's not only the scenery you miss by going too fast — you also miss the sense of where you are going and why." Eddie Cantor

"You must be so busy!" People would always say this to me. I would wear it like a badge of honor. Like there was some award for being the *most* busy! I would have "things to do" in the bathroom, "things to do" in the car and "things to do" in my purse to make use of extra time during unexpected waits.

I think I was born lacking something — I just don't have that "nothing" spot in my brain. It's just not there. I think Randy got my share of it. When he was gazing out into space, looking thoughtful, I would ask, "What are you thinking about?"

"Nothing."

"Well, you must be thinking about *something*?" I'd pry.

"Nope."

How could he just sit and think about *nothing*?

My mind is a constant buzz of activity and it's thoroughly exhausting and often not all that productive. Four in the morning may yield a thought that just *must* be dealt with. Watching a movie at home cannot be *just* watching a movie; it's a chance to catch up on little things like mending, organizing pictures and answering emails. And bed, well the bed is very elusive. I mean, I can't just *go* to bed, not with so

69

many things that *need* to get done. Just one more thing and then I'll go to bed; one more thing and then I'll be done. It's like a disease — the dreaded "Onemorethingitis." Is it just me or have you noticed that generally, when men are tired, they go to sleep? When women are tired, we just complain about how tired we are. It's really draining!

When you suffer with Onemorethingitis, you assume everyone else suffers from the same ailment, too. It may drive you crazy when other people are *not* running around like crazy. This perpetual busyness does not stop for trains, planes or automobiles. Even on a well deserved family vacation, I was busy scuttling everyone around, getting the family organized, ready to go here and there. That's not nagging coming out of my mouth, it's excitement, isn't it?

"Hurry up guys," I said for the tenth time. My impatience was growing by the minute and my voice couldn't hide it.

Randy pulled me aside. Oh-oh, that's never good.

"We are on *vacation*, where do we have to "hurry up" to go?" he asked.

"Well, we have to hurry up and go…and go…(long, awkward pause)…have fun?" I answered rather lamely.

"That is the silliest thing I've ever heard," he replied. "We are on *vacation*, relax!"

Oh. Good point.

Pause. Reflect.

Enlightening strikes again.

Sometimes Enlightening sends other people to strike you. It's really annoying when it sends your husband.

Breathe. Inhale *peace;* hold; exhale *calm.* Repeat. It did feel sort of good. I rubbed my hands together and then cupped them over my eyes for a few minutes. I let the darkness and warmth that my hands provide sooth my tired eyes. Mmm, I should do this more often, I thought. I realized that I needed to practice doing nothing for short chunks of time. I needed to get comfy with being bored, for it is often in these quiet moments that the brilliance sneaks in. But it is hard to do nothing when you tie up your identity in your busyness. I knew that the only way to get good at something was to practice. I decided to figure out what made me feel peaceful and incorporate at least one of these things into my day, every day.

I already knew that taking a pulse slows me down. I sometimes take it on myself, but I prefer the pulse of someone else who is calm and knows what I am doing. Otherwise, it's just weird. I don't know if it's a "nurse thing" or if it's completely bizarre no matter your profession, but tapping into Randy's calm energy and slow rhythmic beating settles me down.

I decide to get rid of my watch — who needs it, it just stresses me more. Time clocks were everywhere should I need to check. The feeling of being watch-free was empowering. Strangely, I felt *more* in control of my time and developed a remarkably accurate sense of time — I'm usually off by only a few minutes.

I realized that I need to practice patience, too. What do patient people do? They don't get upset in long lines; they let other drivers merge into traffic. They aren't always in a hurry; they seem happier. I decided to emulate the behavior of the people with the characteristics I aspire to have. I would do what they do. I would silence the negative self-talk that constantly repeats: "I am just not the patient type, never have been, never will be." Shhh. Every time I did something that patient people did, I would congratulate myself and know that every day I would become more patient, too.

What else could I do? I decided to stop using the "B" word. In my mind the word "busy" has a depressing connotation; I associated it with stress, pressure, negativism. I decided right then and there that I would never be "busy" again. Well, I would never use the *word* busy again. I would use steady, instead. Steady feels calm, in balance, in control. I like steady. Go ahead and ask when you see me, "Are you busy?" "Nope," I will say, "nice and steady, just the way I like it."

Our vacation slowed down to a nice steady pace, because when Momma is calm, everyone's calm. This is not easy work, but I know it's worth it.

REPLACE A WORD THAT IS
NOT SERVING YOU WELL
(LIKE BUSY) WITH ONE
THAT IS MORE POSITIVE AND
PRO-ACTIVE (LIKE STEADY).

Mud On My Soul

"Lean firmly and consistently toward your vision for your life, in the company of those who will celebrate your progress."
Steph

While running through our local city park, I decided to veer off course and try some off-road trails. I soon discovered that going off the beaten path wasn't a great idea. It had rained the entire day before and I made a beeline to get back to the road, but with every step I took, more wet mud caked to the soles of my shoes. Each stride got heavier and heavier due to the weight of the mud and my pleasant jog, suddenly, wasn't so pleasant.

Once on the road I was able to scrape off the mud and continue. Suddenly each step felt even lighter than before.

Enlightening is coming quicker now, more often, and in silly places, through unusual channels, like my runners.

I continued on my run. I got to thinking that the weight of that mud on my shoes was a lot like all the extra "stuff" we carry around with us: things like emotional baggage, old stories that we love to retell but that don't serve us well any more, people who drag us down, negative thoughts that turn into self-fulfilling prophecies, or the negative input we allow into our life in general.

They all bring us down and act as burdens that prevent us from living our life, unlimited. I want as little mud on my soul as possible, so I can do the most good on this earth.

Maybe it's time to get some of the mud off my soul for good. I have been noticing that as I am getting happier, some other people aren't. There are people in my life with whom I feel I cannot share good news. Is this normal? There are people in my life who I feel tired just thinking about. There are people in my life who rarely say anything positive, and it drains me. There are people in my life who always have drama and seem to enjoy it.

Instead of playing their game, I choose instead to fill my dance card with people who fuel me, who support me and in whose life I can make a positive difference.

Of course, while some people are easy to cut the ties with, others are much harder. Sometimes, it so happens that you are married to, are related to, or even gave birth to one of these people. While these close relationships make severing ties impossible, there are rules you can put in place:

Determine and keep a "save yourself" distance.

Establish and stick to clear boundaries about what you will and will not tolerate.

Honor your own personal commitment and choice not to be sucked back into the vortex.

If you are looking to attract more positive people into your life, go hang out where positive people do. Take initiative in connecting with people you think are interesting; be bold and invite someone out for coffee. Have a get together; invite your great people to invite *their* great people to expand your circle.

Most importantly, make sure that the vibes you are sending out are in direct alignment with the ones you want to be attracting.

LOOK AT ATTITUDES OF THE PEOPLE YOU SPEND THE MOST TIME WITH. I HOPE YOU LIKE THEM, BECAUSE CHANCES ARE GOOD YOURS WILL END UP VERY MUCH THE SAME!

Surprise, Surprise, Surprise!

"Just because he doesn't like surprises, doesn't mean I can't have any!" Steph

I love surprises; Randy does not. I spent the first many years of our marriage waiting for a surprise to materialize, to no avail. I spent the next many years explaining that I loved surprises. Nothing. I spent the next many years complaining that I never got surprised.

As every woman knows, it isn't about the gift itself, it is about all the thought and effort and time and care that goes into orchestrating the surprise. Randy always wanted a list for special occasions. He wanted to know what I wanted; he wanted to know what to buy and where to get it. I had this idea that if he really *knew* me, that if he really *loved* me, he would know what I wanted.

Until, surprise, **Enlightening** struck twice.

First, I realized that if Randy was nice enough to ask what I wanted, I should tell him. That year was a Christmas I will never forget because Randy was so happy. He knew he'd gotten it right after looking in store after store with a specific gift in mind. I was not surprised, but I was happy that he was so happy, and he was happy that I was happy, and that sure beats us both being unhappy!

78

Secondly, if you like surprises and you aren't getting any, why not be the giver of surprises? By being the "surpriser," I got to pick surprises that I found fun and was excited about, plus I got the added pleasure of doing something nice for someone else. From then on, I made that my mission and I planned great, fun things. We had an impromptu night in a fancy hotel; we went hang-gliding; we took a trip to Vegas that Randy didn't know about until two hours before departure. I've even thrown myself a few parties. Just because my husband's not the party-throwing type, doesn't mean I still can't have one. Sometimes I even invite him!

It's not the perfect solution, but it sure beats being angry and upset and him feeling bad. It works for us.

Pushing past the stubborn, "he should know" attitude made our relationship stronger and happier. Does this give you any ideas for your relationships?

PEOPLE CAN'T READ YOUR MIND,
EVEN IF THEY LOVE YOU A LOT.
ASK FOR WHAT YOU NEED/WANT;
EVERYONE WILL BE HAPPIER!

A Peek into the Past

"If there is no passion in your life, then have you really lived? Find your passion, whatever it may be. Become it, and let it become you and you will find great things happen for you, to you and because of you." T. Allen Armstrong

One seemingly insignificant comment can change your world, even when you are least expecting it.

What was the name of that sweet boy in junior high? You know, the one you eyed and thought was so cute, the one who saw you as a buddy even though you were hoping for something more? Mike was that boy to me. While some people choose a high school for its music program or its sports teams or its academics, I chose mine because of Mike. If it was good enough for him, it was good enough for me.

I don't remember how I rationalized to my parents why I needed to go to a school out of our area, but I must have been convincing because I spent the next four years there, with my buddy Mike. I wouldn't know the significance of our relationship for a long, long time.

I was delighted to bump into "my" Mike again, many years later, at a local burger joint. We were having a pleasant chat to reminisce and catch up. And then he said the words that

changed everything, "Hey, Steph, do you still write poetry?"
Write *poetry*?

I was taken aback. I had not written or even thought about
writing poetry in ages. I cannot even remember telling
anyone, let alone a male friend, that I penned rhyming words
in my spare time. I wondered how on earth he remembered.
Oh my God, I thought, I hope I didn't write him something
embarrassing!

But now that you mention it, I had *loved* writing back then.
Writing was my lifeline in high school; it was my outlet, my
safe place. With my words I could escape, problem solve and
make some sense of my world. Writing came easily and
effortlessly to me and was a great way to relieve the stress of
being a teenager; it just felt good to put those words onto
paper.

Mike's simple question gnawed at me as the week went
on until the bolt of **Enlightening** finally hit me with this
question: When and why did I stop writing?

There are always reasons why we don't pursue our passions:
not enough time, not enough money, too old, too young, too
heavy, or the fear that we can't do it as well as we used to.

But there are just as many reasons (maybe more!) *to* pursue
our passions:

- To create happy feelings

- To make us more interesting

- To have fun

- To leave us feeling fulfilled

- To help us feel alive

- To relieve stress

- To allow us to share our gifts and talents with the world

For all these reasons we must *choose* to put cultivating our passions on our priority list.

If you are fortunate enough to know what you are passionate about now, you must look for ways to experience and express it more. If you can't think of a passion at present, looking back into your past to what you used to love is a good place to start. Pay attention to things you are doing when time passes very quickly. Pay attention to what section of the bookstore you go to first or what part of the paper you read first. These things may give you a clue to things you love. Even if you can't do whatever it is at the same level anymore, you can still be part of the game, the choir, or the event in some capacity. Maybe you could coach, mentor, teach or share your passion with someone else. Maybe it's not lowering the bar; maybe it's just adjusting the bar.

As I thought more about rediscovering my love for writing, I decided that if one passion was good, maybe two or three

82

would be even better. How would I know what I was passionate about *now* unless I got out and tried new things and had new experiences? I decided to be aware of new opportunities that could lead me to a brand new passion. Meanwhile, I would make time in my life to write. I would try to write every day. I would reclaim my passion for writing; maybe someday I would even write a book.

While thinking about passion, I started to think about my career. Was I passionate about my job? Was I passionate about my profession? I loved helping people and felt that what I was doing mattered, but I also had the feeling that something was not quite right. While I knew that nobody loved *everything* about their job, I still thought that loving it 80 per cent of the time was a reasonable expectation. Did I love 80 per cent of my job?

Do you have a passion? Would you like to start exploring to find one? Do you love 80 per cent of your work?

YOUR PASSION IS WAITING TO BE DISCOVERED! IF YOU DON'T HAVE SOMETHING YOU ARE PASSIONATE ABOUT RIGHT NOW (BESIDES FAMILY AND WORK), GET OUT MORE AND TRY NEW THINGS!

P.S.   Here is a poem that I wrote as a "wise" 17-year-old. Don't laugh!

As Time Goes On

As time goes on you learn to accept

The past, as it was and you learn to accept

The heartaches, the defeat, the tears

And you start to realize

That the memories do have meaning

And that the meaning of the memories

Are the keys to the future.

As time goes on

You learn that you are strong

That you can get up and start all over.

You learn to appreciate

All of the good and to anticipate

Some of the bad

So that you will be prepared.

As time goes on

You learn the more difficult

You make life for other people

The more difficult you make it for yourself.

And as time goes on

You will learn to go on and on

Coping with the things and taking in stride the things

That you will learn to accept

As time goes on.

Bacon Rules?

"To effectively communicate, we must realize that we are all different in the way we perceive the world and use this understanding as a guide to our communication with others." Anthony Robbins

Some people think it's hard to be married; I disagree. I think the challenge comes in being *happily* married. Anyone can rack up years of staying together, but to be happy after all those years, to still enjoy each other's company, to get excited when you see your spouse's car in the driveway — now that's different.

Whatever your relationship status is, sometimes, probably most times, it just doesn't pay to argue. But then again sometimes, grrrr, things just drive you crazy. If you have a pretty good handle on the big issues in your relationship, like money, parenting and sex, it's usually the little things that grate on your nerves.

Now I love my husband; he is smart and funny and kind. But sometimes, he is very stubborn. I guess we have that in common. Year after year, Randy and I have had the same discussion and never once has a resolution come around. The issue at hand? Bacon grease.

How do *you* dispose of bacon grease?

She said: "When I was growing up my parents put it in a container and froze it, then later when it had solidified threw it in the garbage." (Clearly the proper way.)

He said: "When I was growing up my parents ran hot water down the drain, poured the grease down, ran some more hot water and then it was gone. My Dad was a plumber and he said as long as you ran the hot water there was no concern for the pipes." (Gasp! Seems like a waste of water to me!)

Every time we had bacon, without fail, the bacon disposal discussion came into play. Neither of us would budge. Both of us had a deep belief that our method was the right way, and would cringe when the wrong disposal technique was used.

Tired of ruining our weekend breakfasts, we knew that we either had to come up with some kind of resolution, or stop having bacon, which was, although a good idea for health reasons, not a viable option.

 Every now and then you can just ask for **Enlightening** point blank, and an answer will appear.

For us, the solution was to agree to disagree. So we made a deal: if I was cleaning up, I got to dispose of it my way and he would shut up. If he was cleaning up, he would dispose of it his way and I would have to shut up.

And so was developed the "Bacon Grease Accord."

Agreeing to disagree leaves feelings, relationships and respect intact. I cannot expect others to think like me, no matter how right I think I am. I understand that there is usually more than one right answer to any given issue. Even if I don't value the idea, I value the person; so there is much value in *respecting* the idea. Thanks to the Bacon Grease Accord, I realized that everything that I said in my head did not need to be said out loud. This realization had led to greater harmony, peace and contentment in my home, and in the rest of my life in general.

I know that it seems like the words you think, but don't say, will cause you to explode, but trust me, they won't. Remember that you can't put toothpaste back in the tube! You are aiming for uncommon success and this relationship-saving information is so important!

TO MAKE ANY RELATIONSHIP BETTER, KNOW THAT EVERYTHING IN YOUR HEAD DOES NOT NEED TO BE SAID.

A Life-Changing Golf Game

"Live so that when your children think of fairness, caring and integrity, they think of you." H. Jackson Brown, Jr.

What a great way to bond with the girlfriends, on our local nine-hole golf course, chatting it up, enjoying the weather and not keeping score (we have a lot more fun that way)! These outings were a good way to spend time outdoors and visit while getting a little exercise; golfing was really secondary. Cindy was telling me about her upcoming plans to go to the East Coast to visit her family, and she said she would be going with her youngest son, Ian. "Oh, wow," I said rather surprised, "what about Mark?"

Cindy had another son and I wondered how he felt about her just taking his younger brother on a vacation? To me it didn't seem fair. "Mark knows this is Ian's turn to come on a trip," Cindy replied matter of factly. "Next year will be his turn and he's okay with that." Huh?

Enlightening strikes.

Although this was a very foreign concept to me, I recognized that it was a great idea (and all great ideas don't have to be mine). I had always tried to keep things equal between my three kids. In fact, I had tried so hard to keep things equal that we all missed out on opportunities. We could rarely afford to take all of the kids somewhere, so we just didn't go. What would it be like if I implemented Cindy's strategy?

This jolt of enlightening has been the impetus for many wonderful adventures with my kids. Sometimes one of them will accompany me on a business trip, or we will partner with a friend and her child to go to a beach cabin close to home. These trips, mini-trips and even ice cream dates have become irreplaceable part of our family construct.

I have had the same conversation with others that Cindy had with me those many years ago, and the response is often the same. I know that Cindy's story has inspired many others to put *quality time* above *equality time*, whether it's with their partners, children, grandchildren or extended families. Does it give you any ideas?

SOMETIMES WE TRY SO
HARD TO BE EQUAL,
WE AREN'T BEING FAIR.

Tall Poppies

"I love surprises and coincidences. I love them even more when I don't pass them off as luck, but rather recognize them as a sign that my life's course is right on track." Jason Mraz

A special couple was coming upon a significant wedding anniversary. When talking about their plans to celebrate, the wife said they were going to renew their vows, but then decided that they just couldn't, out of respect for their friends. So many of their friends were unhappily married, she said, going though separations or divorces, that they didn't want to "rub their noses in it." She viewed the celebration of their milestone as something that would make others uncomfortable or unhappy. I guess that's one way to look at things.

This was clearly a case of Tall Poppy Syndrome. It's barbaric really! The story goes that a tall poppy grows in the field amidst the other poppies, but it looks tall and out of place, so it is chopped down to make all the poppies look the same.

Often in life, we don't want to stand out and be acknowledged for what we do well. We want to be like all the other "poppies" because it's uncomfortable for most of us to stand up straight. We belittle ourselves; we toss back compliments that come our way; we make light of what we have done; we attribute our successes to luck; we give credit to everyone else. Maybe we don't renew our vows because we don't want others to feel bad.

I rather like it when I can learn from someone else's **Enlightening** strike.

If we choose to shift our perspective on this issue, we might see that if we stand tall, we might encourage others to do the same — to raise their bars, to aspire to levels that they may not have considered before. We might give them hope that they too can have more, do more, be more, if they choose.

Tall poppies unite! Let's create acres and acres of us and create a new norm. Let's encourage others to stand up and stand out and recognize their greatness, too!

To do this, you must start from within. When you do something great, own it; be proud and share your strategies for success. This does not mean you will become a vain, egotistical, boastful person; it means you are acknowledging your contributions to the world and inspiring others to do the same. How can we share our gifts if we don't recognize them?

P.S. My friends haven't renewed their vows…yet!

NEVER BE AFRAID TO
LET YOUR LIGHT SHINE,
IT LIGHTS THE
WAY FOR OTHERS.

Beautiful Apples

"If service is the rent you pay for your existence on this earth, are you behind in your rent?" Robert G. Allen

I have two fantastic apple trees in my backyard. Every second year they produce the most amazing big, sweet, juicy, tasty apples. I slice, dice and bake them, but there are only so many apples one family can enjoy, right?

When an acquaintance of mine heard of my apple overload he remarked, "I will take some. I go out and pick apples to bring to the food bank and the homeless shelters." What a great idea!

It wasn't long before he and his wife came over and gathered a big box of apples. They were delighted; I was delighted, and I was certain those who received the apples would be delighted too.

When next I spoke with this fellow, I asked how the apples went over.

"Oh, they were beautiful and delicious! My family really enjoyed them," he said excitedly.

"Great, how did they like them at the homeless shelter?" I asked.

"Oh," he said, "I didn't take them there; they were too nice to take there; I gave them away to my friends and family instead."

I beg your pardon? They were *too* nice to give away? Did I hear that right?

I could have given them to my family and friends, but I gave them to *him* because he was going to share them with the less fortunate — that was the whole point, wasn't it?

 This really got me steamed and something about steam brings on **Enlightening.**

Suddenly, a little voice in the back of my head said, "Hello, Stephanie, excuse me, I seem to remember that you said, "that's too good to give away" in regards to giving away used clothing or household items."

Uhhh, right. Busted.

Metaphorically speaking, do the less fortunate only deserve bruised apples? Do they only deserve sour apples? Do they only deserve torn, worn and used clothes? Do they only deserve the stuff that is "bad enough" for them, items we don't deem "good enough" for ourselves?

Why not give it away? If we can't use it, don't use it, won't use it, don't love it. If it doesn't bring *us* joy, then let's give it away, even if, especially if, it is good. The less fortunate deserve "beautiful apples" just as much as we do, maybe more. They would probably appreciate them more, too. True charity doesn't matter if it's tax deductible. True generosity is not giving away something that you don't want anymore, but giving away something you do want.

I suppose a few apples are a small price to pay for a new outlook on philanthropy. I will adopt the "poor-man philanthropy" philosophy: we can do big amounts of good with little amounts of money or time. On grocery shopping day, I can push the cart down the baby food isle and pick up a few jars for the food bank; I can give blood; I can buy extra school supplies; I can share what we have. Hmm…I suddenly have this strong urge to de-clutter.

(An added bonus: Apparently, there is a direct correlation between de-cluttering and losing weight!)

Giving – it feels good, it feels right.

IF YOU DON'T LOVE IT,
IF IT DOESN'T BRING YOU JOY
OR IF IT'S NOT USEFUL TO YOU,
GIVE IT AWAY TO SOMEONE ELSE.

No Breaky

"I'm in a hurry to get things done, I rush and rush until life's no fun. All I really gotta do is live and die, I'm in a hurry and don't know why." Alabama

Mornings — you either love 'em or you hate 'em.

For me, trying to get three kids out the door for school, four pets settled before being left alone, and two adults to work on time proved to be a Monday to Friday "daymare." I came to dread this morning rush; it felt like the clock was ruling my life. Even during my morning shower, before the "rush" started, I could feel the knot of stress in my stomach as I thought about what still had to get done. It was a dine and dash scenario of wake up, dress up, eat up and *go*! It was a cacophony of yelling and barking, a muddle of forgetting things and dashing back. Sure enough though, every morning, lunches were packed, forms were signed and little people, big people and pets got to where they needed to be at the appointed times. I don't know how they felt when they got to where they were going, but I wasn't feeling so hot. By 10 a.m., as the adrenaline wore off, I felt the adverse affects of our non-productive, morning habits.

I found myself feeling fatigued and famished. In my rush to get everyone else ready, I always forgot to get myself ready, rarely remembering to eat. Then I was hungry, cranky and resentful, feeling like I was the last thing on the morning "to-do" list.

Repeat same story the next day, and the next, and the next, and the next.

ALRIGHT, JUST RELAX!
EVERYBODY WILL GET A TURN.
NOW WHICH BOLT WAS HERE FIRST?

Enlightening enters this time in the form of questions: "Is this what you want to teach your kids? Is this how you want your daughters to raise their families? Is this how you want your son to see women function — to do for others constantly, to never sit down, to forget to feed themselves?"

In my haste to take care of everyone and everything, I was modeling exactly what I didn't want my kids to do when they were adults. Things had to change. Mornings were going to start getting a little better at the Staples house. Unfortunately, things had to get a little worse first.

Six words strung together by Steven Covey changed everything for me: *"Begin with the end in mind."* My "end," in this case, was having a morning that was relaxed, pleasant, organized and *calm.* I began to work backwards from there. What could I do to make those things a reality?

The first step was preparation. We needed to be more organized the night before so that chaos wouldn't ensue in the morning. We also needed to enlist the children, having them do as much for themselves as possible, with me to guide, but *not* to do. The primary change was that they would begin to make their own lunches the night before. This was met with a fair amount a resistance, as they pointed out to me *no one* in their classes made their own lunches, that *everyone's* Mother did it for them.

They got over it and eventually they even felt some pride in being able to do for themselves and have some control over what went in their lunches (I still stuffed in a note, joke or cartoon strip here and there). The next step was purchasing alarm clocks for everyone. No longer would I be the nasty one who had to drag them out of bed — Mr. Alarm Clock got that job. A firm breakfast time was set and everyone was expected to be at the table at that time. The time they got up depended on how long they needed to get ready before the "Big Breakfast." I woke up 15 minutes earlier than usual and prepared a decent breakfast and we all sat down and ate together — how novel!!

Sometimes we even read a short, inspirational story from one of the *Chicken Soup for the Soul* books. Those short stories provided not only a forum for discussion but also a really nice start to the day. Needless to say, mornings became a whole lot nicer around our place, and I became a whole lot nicer too. I think the kids grew a little on the inside and our family was strengthened by this new resolve. My 15 minutes less sleep was well worth the payoff of having a relaxed, pleasant, organized and calm morning we enjoyed as a family.

In the case of the harried mornings asking myself, "Is this what I want my kids to emulate when they have a family?" was the impetus I needed to make change happen.

RECOGNIZE THE MOST STRESSFUL TIME OF YOUR DAY AND PURPOSEFULLY PLAN A STRATEGY TO MAKE IT MORE PEACEFUL.

Do What You Have To Do

"Instinct is the nose of the mind." Madame De Girardin

Pivotal moments in life stand out. Some subtleties are etched in stone, frozen in time. For me, the day I learned about an emerging profession called Life Coaching was one of those moments.

By this time, my personal reinvention was well under way. I was happy; I had a great life, and most days I quite liked being me. I was hooked on personal growth because I had seen it work its magic first-hand. Then some people asked me about it. What did I do? How did I do it? Could I help them too? And poof, like an answer to a question I hadn't even asked, there it was in a magazine, an article about something called Life Coaching.

I felt an instant attraction, a deep knowing, a pull. I was compelled to research, investigate and explore this interesting new profession. It sounded fascinating; it felt like an ideal fit. It seemed, well, perfect! I would be able to use my passion and would definitely love 80 per cent of this job. Still I resisted. After all, I had a perfectly fine career as a nurse. Why would I trade security and stability for the unsure and unknown? Ridiculous! But the idea wouldn't let go of me; it had a tight hold and I couldn't get it out of my mind. I didn't know what to do next.

Sometimes Enlightening whispers; sometimes it is so subtle you barely feel a thing. Sometimes you sense it, but you ignore it; you shove it down. *"Pay attention,"* it nudges.

They say when you are ready to learn the teacher appears, and so it was that I met Benita.

Benita is a red-headed wonder. She is charming and fun and helpful and wow, she is excited about life! She is also very generous with her time. At the time, she was perhaps the only Life Coach in our city, and she offered to coach me for free so I could see for myself how powerful the experience could be. She told me that even if I didn't coach a single person, the training would improve my own life so much that it would be well worth the investment. I believed her and she became my personal coach and mentor.

The personal coaching was an experience like no other, and I was shocked and thrilled by the results. If I had done this sooner, I thought, then it surely would not have taken me this long to get this far. As a coach, Benita was my champion, my partner, and my sounding board. I was hooked!

♪ Zing — **Enlightening** Strikes

Intuition is a powerful tool. When my head is too logical and my heart is too soft, I need to pay more attention to this knowing, this gut feeling, this intuition. I know I will never go "coach-less" again and to the core of my being, I know what I have to do. Now how do I tell Randy I want to leave my well paying, secure, benefit-laden job for a career he has never even heard of?

TO GO FURTHER,
FASTER AND EASIER,
GET A COACH, CHAMPION,
PARTNER OR MENTOR
ON YOUR TEAM.

Part Three – Your Life, Unlimited

The Coach Approach

"To decide is to walk facing forward with nary a crick in your neck from looking back at the crossroads." Betsy Cañas Garmon

If there is one thing we adults don't do enough of, it's party. Our life is so serious: work, taxes, bills, dentists, home repairs, blah, blah, blah. We need to have fun more often. What if we had frequent parties for any crazy reason at all? How about an "I need to clean my house party," a "The kids are back in school party," a "My adult children moved out of my house party," or in my case, an "I have a big announcement party."

I don't even need **Enlightening** to strike to tell me that I cannot do this new career thing alone. I need my partner, family and friends, my "dream team" on board. I throw a big party and invite everyone I love. They know I have a big announcement and they speculate that I am pregnant. Funny, very funny.

"I am changing careers," I surprise them.

"I am going to be a Life Coach," I announce with an equal mix of trepidation and sheer delight. Picture a big room with lots of quiet people. No one said a thing. Finally one of my friends breaks the silence, "I have no idea what that is, but I bet you'll be great at it!"

"Oh, yes, I think so too," everyone concurs, unsure but happy for me nonetheless.

You just can't buy friends like that. They have no clue what you are doing, but they support you anyway.

Establishing new friendships and making old ones even better has been one of the best side effects of my reinvention. Gone are the folks in whose presence I felt small. Gone are those individuals who suck the life out of me and who brought only negative energy into the room and into my life. Gone are the people who thrive on bad news and cannot share in the delight of good news.

It happened slowly. It was almost a case of natural selection, as if it was the only way it really could be. I seem to repel those negative people now and I find that sort of humorous. They don't really want to be around me anymore. Maybe they were scared of what was happening. Maybe they were afraid they would have to change, too?

That's okay, because in their place are wonderful, supportive, happy, optimistic, pro-active people. I know my growth is in direct proportion to the quality of the new people in my life.

Back to the party. The least I can do is fill my partygoers in on this mysterious vocation.

"I am going to work with people who want to get more out of life, who want to live better, dream bigger, reach higher. I am going to be their cheerleader, champion, partner and coach. I know you have never heard of coaching, but just wait, in five years, everyone will have a coach, know a coach or be a coach."

And that is exactly what happened. Coaching has boomed and for good reason. *Everybody* can benefit from an objective partner in their corner whose only motive is to help them enrich their life through personal development and growth.

People sometimes comment that I made such a huge shift in careers. I disagree. The essence of nursing is about helping people and the essence of coaching is exactly the same.

I am so thankful to my dream team for supporting me in this new business. My personal growth and life enrichment coaching practice called, "Your Life, Unlimited" is born!

If you are waiting for the perfect time to make that important decision — ta-da — the perfect time is now!

INDECISION IS, IN ITSELF, A DECISION.

It's Not a Matter of *If*, It's a Matter of *When* (revisited)

"Talking is like playing on the harp; there is as much in laying the hands on the strings to stop their vibration as in twanging them to bring out their music." *Oliver Wendell Holmes*

I am breezing through my kid's school, when this older gentleman grabs my arm.

"Steph!" he says, in an enthusiastic voice.

"Yes?" I reply with a blank look in my eyes.

"Don't you know who I am?" he says, sounding crushed.

I look this man up and down for a moment. I lower my eyebrows and cock my head, and then I look deep into his eyes. The dots slowly connect in my head. And finally, in voice with an inflection I cannot adequately describe on paper, I say, "Dave?"

"Yep!" he says happily and he confirms my suspicions.

In that same tone I heard from him on my doorstep many years before, I say, "Ohhh, Dave."

This was not the Dave I remembered, with the biceps, the uniform and the horse. My, my.

And me…well, I guess God felt sorry for me after the last encounter because that day, I was looking about as good as I get. I was dressed up, made up, shaped up and "happied" up. All was right with my world. One of us was having some "issues" and this time it wasn't me!

106

Hmmm, what do you know? See me smiling on the inside, bad me.

But not so fast, my house of cards was about to fall.

We started talking. I should say *he* started talking and he was asking me questions – a lot of questions. Difficult questions like: What do you do? Where do you live? How old are your kids? Tough stuff, I'm telling you.

That's when everything went into that slow motion movie speed again, and that's never good.

I was tongue tied. I could not speak. No, I *really* could not speak. I literally could not wrap my lips around a coherent sentence. I don't know if it was the shock of seeing him again, or what, but I could not speak. My mouth was gaping open as if poised to catch flies.

I stuttered, I stumbled, I stammered. Nothing lucid came out of my mouth, nothing but incoherent babble. I can't even imagine what he thought.

Again, we parted, leaving me totally discombobulated.

Arghhh! Come on now, Enlightening; I know you are coming with something, but what? I'm taking care of myself and I'm doing well. What on earth was this all about? I see the humiliation again, but where's the learning here this time?

I'm waiting. You're killing me here. What *is* it?

Sometimes when you want Enlightening, it doesn't come. What a bummer!

Sometimes, even when you are looking for Enlightening, you can't find it. Go figure.

Sometimes, there just doesn't seem to be any sense at all to what happens, but not this time. This time I finally figure it out.

 Ka-pow, **Enlightening** strikes with one big, bold word: Toastmasters.

I needed to learn how to think on the spot, converse during stressful periods and communicate effectively and eloquently. Toastmasters, the international organization designed to help people improve their speaking, communication and leadership skills was my destination. Dave was just my compass to point me there.

If a little humiliation is what it takes to grow, then bring it on!

I research clubs in my area and find one that fits my life. I excitedly immerse myself into the world of Toastmasters. It is the most effective, and cost efficient, personal growth avenue I have found. I don't know anyone who wouldn't benefit from all that it offers. Not only that, other people who recognize and are interested in the benefits of personal growth go there; so great people abound! I am a fan for life. And guess what, it worked!

It helped me become more confident and capable; it helped me learn to think on my feet and stretch my boundaries; it helped me to become better organized and more creative. All this happened in a safe environment with people who wanted to help me be a better me. As with anything, the more you put into Toastmasters, the more you get out of it.

By now I had been enjoying doing personal coaching, group coaching and teaching adult education coaching classes for our local school division. Out of the blue, a client asked me if I would lead a seminar on personal growth for her conference.

Well, I had never done that before, but with Toastmasters in my back pocket, I was sure I could do it.

And so it was that I began to get paid to share my message about harnessing the power of personal growth — unbelievable!

How could *you* benefit from improving your communication and leadership skills? How would others in your world benefit from your learning?

DON'T ASK IF YOU CAN USE THIS INFORMATION, ASK HOW CAN I USE THIS INFORMATION.

I Hate It When He's Right

"I have not been successful in life if my friends or family think I am too busy for them." Steph

My great friend Gloria popped in one day shortly before suppertime. We talked as she sat and had a glass of iced tea. I thought it would be a good use of time to unload the dishwasher while we were chatting. As I opened the dishwasher, Randy closed it with his foot, telling me subtly without words, that this was not the time to do that.

"He's right," I thought as I continued the visit with my friend. I got myself a glass and sat down with her.

Later that evening, while I was working in my office Randy came in and sat down. Oh-oh.

"You know I closed that dishwasher door when Gloria was here because it's not polite to do chores while your friends are visiting."

"Yes, you're right, thank you," I told him.

"When did he get so wise?" I wondered silently.

He went on, "In fact, the other day when Dawn was over, she was talking to you at the front door, and then you started straightening out the shoes in the doorway. You do this kind of thing quite often."

♪ DZIT, DZIT — **Enlightening**, welcome back; I missed you there for the short time you were gone.

Oh my, he was right again (I hate that!). In my effort to be ultra efficient, I was being a poor listener and rude, to boot.

What am I telling my friends, nonverbally, when I do this kind of thing? That my time is so precious, I cannot spend a few minutes listening, sitting, visiting with people I care about? That I must be doing, doing, doing, instead of just being? Am

110

I not valuing our relationship enough to give it my undivided attention?

Just when I think no one is really noticing, I realize that I am wrong. People are very observant, not only to what you are saying, but to what you are doing, to how you are acting, to how you are *being*. In fact, some research indicates that multitasking may weaken cognitive ability. Hmmm…I probably cannot afford this.

I acknowledge that sometimes multitasking is a must, but not nearly as often as I think it is. Health care studies show that patients *perceive* the nurse is spending more time with them if the nurse simply sits down with them. I bet this is not just true in health care. I bet if I sat down with my husband, my kids and my friends, it would give the same message: I care about you, you are valuable to me, I want to spend this time with you.

If it's really impossible to talk at this time, I will explain that I really want to give them 100 per cent of my attention and then give them a couple of choices of times when they can have it. I know I have time for the most important people in my life. I need to make sure the people I love know that too.

I will challenge myself to be a more attentive listener. The dishes and the shoes will still be there. What relationship of yours would benefit if you listened more attentively?

YOU DON'T HAVE TO SOLVE EVERYONE ELSE'S PROBLEMS; YOU JUST HAVE TO LISTEN ATTENTIVELY AND CARE DEEPLY.

Braces Anyone?

"Argument is the worst sort of conversation." Jonathan Swift

I was yelling and screaming at my teenage daughter. We were standing in the hallway beside the full length closet mirrors and she stared at me for a long time before she finally said, in a very calm voice, "Mom. Mom, look at yourself in the mirror." I will never forget that frightening sight. I was out of control and we both knew it.

The orthodontist said braces were optional, but recommended for my youngest daughter, Gina, and she was not convinced she wanted to get them. She kept putting off making a decision and to tell you the truth, I sort of forgot about it too. One day I stumbled upon the paperwork and realized we needed to decide, pronto.

I called to Gina and said, "We need to decide about these braces, right now."

This began a long, difficult argument and ended with my having a, well, what should I call it; a screaming fit, a meltdown, an adult equivalent of a temper tantrum and generally losing it. It was bad. It was about as opposite from uncommon success as you can get.

I wish her little comment woke me up but it only made me angrier. My husband came up to rescue us both and he took my daughter to her room to deal properly with the issue.

I was left alone and raging. I didn't know what to do with myself, so I went out into the garage and screamed. I screamed and cried and cried and screamed. I screamed until I had no more voice, and I cried until I had no more tears. When the tirade was done and I had nothing left, I sunk into a ball of despair.

I remember having the presence of mind to think two things: first, how is it that I can help other people, but I can't help my own daughter? Secondly, it was a good thing I wasn't speaking the next day because I have just killed my voice.

Enlightening quietly wrapped its arms around me, gently, kindly, forgivingly. It sat with me while I tried to catch my breath and regain my composure. It stayed while I realized that I could help my daughter by helping myself. It showed me that I was in dire need of some new skills.

Whatever issue is pressing, know that you are not alone. Just when you think you have tried everything, know there is one more thing to try right around the corner. There is always someone else who has had the same problem (probably worse), someone who has written a book about the solution, someone who is teaching a course on how to handle it or someone that has a resource to share with you. Once we identify the problem, then we can look for solutions. If we are open to seeking advice and counsel, the support from others can be a lifeline. Resources abound: library, internet, connections, bookstores or in person classes — offering new insights into old problems. They are all readily available.

This time I found my answer online. I discovered this simple two-step communication tool called "intent and consent," within a great work from Dennis Rivers called *The Seven Challenges*. It works like this: Step one: State the intention of your conversation, that is, what you need to talk about and approximately how long you will need. Step two: Establish a good time to talk and get the consent of the other person.

The more important the conversation, the more important intent and consent is, because it gives the other person time to consider the situation and prepare. You are more likely to then have the other person come to the table willingly.

Here is how this technique could have been used when I discovered the paperwork for the braces: "Gina, I need to talk to you about your braces. We are going to have to make some sort of decision really soon. It will probably take about 15 minutes to lay out our options. After supper, either tonight or tomorrow, we will need to discuss this. Which of those times would work better for you?'

In the end, I apologized to my daughter for handling the situation so poorly, I forgave myself for being human, and safely tucked the intent and consent tool into my communications kit, near the top so I could easily pull it out for future use.

Ask yourself who would appreciate it if you implemented intent and consent prior to discussing an issue?

THE MORE IMPORTANT
THE CONVERSATION,
THE MORE IMPORTANT
INTENT AND CONSENT IS.

Rocket Science

"When the world says, "Give up," Hope whispers, "Try it one more time." Author Unknown

I am really loving my coaching, and the speaking: it's amazing how they both fuel me. By now it is clear that I have a message, a message about empowering yourself and enriching your life. People want, perhaps even *need* to hear it. How can I get more people to hear this message?

 Ka Boom — **Enlightening** strikes up a conversation with me. What about Radio?

Radio? Yes, radio.

I don't know a thing about radio, says mini-me, the me who comes out when I am not thinking big. Then I ask myself:

Do you have a message you believe in? Yes.

Do you think radio would be a vehicle for more people to benefit from this message? Yes.

Why not give it a shot then? Because I have no experience in radio broadcasting, journalism or communications, that's why.

And...? And the powers that be won't let me past the gate.

Why not try it anyway — you have been right a time or two before. Well, maybe the university radio station has some air time they want to get rid of.

What would you do if you were 10 times bolder?

I decided I would start with the number one most listened to station, I think, trying on the "bold" cloak. I found the contact information for the program director at CJOB, our local talk radio station and I made the call.

115

"I have a great idea for an innovative, inspiring radio show," I say to the answering machine, trying to sound confident. "It is exactly what your radio station needs. Call me!"

And he does; within 24 hours, the program director is on the line.

"Tell me about your idea," Vic says.

Seriously? I was just kidding, actually. I don't *really* want to be on the radio! Mini-me is back.

I tell him my idea and he is interested.

"Send me a format for the show and I'll look it over."

"Sir," I say, "if I knew what a radio format looked like, I would certainly do that."

He explains what it is and I start writing. I stay up all night and write a "format" for my pretend radio show.

Just for fun, here is the exact text from the cover letter I sent with the proposal:

Hello Mr. Grant, (oh, I feel like I just stepped off the Mary Tyler Moore set!)

Thank you for entertaining my proposal for a quality women's program. I am excited by the prospect of being able to bring a fun, engaging and informative radio show to Winnipeg women! Rest assured this will not be an infomercial, I will act as host and facilitator to provide "meat," not "fluff." The show would focus on ways for real women to improve their lives and emphasize other women who model the way.

As a Certified Personal Life Coach, I strive to help my clients bridge the gap between where they are now and where they want to be. It is exciting, rewarding work! I trust you will appreciate my forthright honesty as I have told you, I have absolutely no experience in radio. I do, however bring to the table experience as a nurse, coach, public speaker, mother, wife, daughter and proud (almost) lifelong Winnipegger. I strive to do my best, to live and work with integrity and I pride myself on practicing what I preach: that is, we can "have it all:" personal/work balance and happiness in general.

I understand that the ideas for a radio show must be copious and ongoing to supply fresh, interesting and motivating material to the women of our city, but I believe we have an ABUNDANCE of talent and inspiration right under our very noses. I look forward to the opportunity to uncover them!

Please find attached the proposal for you to peruse, as you requested.

Together, we can make this into a program you will be proud to have your name attached to.

Looking forward to talking to you further!

Sincerely,

Stephanie Staples

I hesitatingly press "send" and I wait, and I wait, and I wait. Nothing.

Mini-me says, "See, I told you."

117

Enlightening says, "Don't stop."

I send another email: "I guess I didn't 'wow' you with that proposal. What does it take to wow you?"

The response: "Haven't read it. Do you know how many proposals I have on my desk? I'll read it next month."

Oh.

Next month comes and goes. Mini-me says, "See. I told you." Enlightening says, "Don't you stop!"

I contact him again, trying to be light. I say, "I haven't heard a 'no' from you yet, so I am just wondering if my proposal is still on the table."

"Come and see me Wednesday at eleven," he responds gruffly.

Wednesday at eleven. Right. I'll be there. Oh dear. Talking to myself is a fine pastime.

Wednesday at eleven, I am at the radio station. Vic, a stout and formidable looking man, is sitting behind his big, mahogany desk, leaning back with his arms crossed. I suspect he has seen and heard it all after forty-odd years in the media. "So you want to be on the radio," he says as more of a statement than a question.

"Not really," I reply honestly. "I just have a message that I know helps people live their lives better and the radio would be a way for more people to hear it."

We talk for twenty minutes. He is impressed that I am a professional speaker and he likes the idea of a positive show, amidst their lineup, especially one that would appeal to women.

"I'll give you six weeks, sink or swim." There is no mistake that I've used up my allotted time.

"Wonderful! Is there a course, a manual, some training I should take?"

"It's not exactly rocket science," he says matter-of-factly.

Not for *you* maybe, you've been doing this for forty years. The only thing *I* know about radio is how to turn it on. I keep these thoughts to myself.

The meeting is over.

I can hardly drive home; I panic. Why do I do these crazy things? Why doesn't someone stop me? Breathe, breathe, breathe. Does anyone have a paper bag?

A few short weeks later, Your Life, Unlimited the radio show goes to air and except for a three second delay — we are live! To save my sanity, I decide to employ a technique called, "What if." What if I was a radio personality? What if I was the most excellent host and interviewer? What if I brought great ideas to people of all ages? What if this show is exactly what so many people need to hear? I take a swig of water, a big breath of air and I press the "on air" button. I pretend I am a radio host.

Vic calls into the studio during the first commercial, "Tell her she's doing great," he tells the producer. Whew. It wasn't rocket science after all and it turned out that this tough program director was quite a marshmallow (and funny), after all. Here is the email he sent after the first show:

Having gone through the same experience a number of years ago, I know breathing was somewhat difficult for you on Saturday starting about 1:58:30 p.m.

It was an excellent start as you endured the nervousness well and sounded knowledgeable and I could tell your confidence was growing with each passing minute. Having said that, getting to the comfort zone is a slow process, so be patient.

My wife listened to the whole show and her thoughts following were: "That was a good show," based somewhat on the fact that she was quite familiar with your guest.

I think you've already noted some of the tips which would be forthcoming: Be yourself; know what you're talking about; and be prepared; always be prepared. It was a good start and as you become more accustomed to the process you'll show ongoing progress.

Stick with me, Kid, one day you'll be famous, or at least known, or at least thought of, or at least familiar to those closest to you.

In summation: I threw you in to sink or swim.....you swam. I don't usually put people into that position if I think they'll sink.

Cheers,

Vic

That was in 2006. I love that radio show; it was so scary then but turned into one of the most fun things I have ever done. I know my show would have never had a chance to be aired without the gift of persistence. In addition to my weekly show, I was invited to do a "Motivation Moment" for the station on weekdays. They call me wherever I am and I share some ideas for better living with the listeners. At first I was worried I would run out of inspiring incidents and ideas, but when you set your radar for insight and inspiration, it doesn't let you down. In fact, no matter what you set your radar for – you are likely to find!

You probably don't want a radio show, but there *is* something that you do want. What is it? What's going on in your world that would benefit from persistence, persistence and more persistence?

WHEN YOU ENCOUNTER SOMETHING THAT IS SCARY OR FOREIGN TO YOU, EMPLOY THE "WHAT IF" TECHNIQUE TO HELP YOU GROW TO GREATER HEIGHTS.

I Won the Lottery!

"My heart went up and then my heart went down. I like my heart better when it's up. Luckily we can put it up any time we want!" Stephanie Staples

"This is Constable Jay, may I speak with Randy Staples."

Hmmm, confusion and a slight amount of worry set in as I took this call. Why is the police department calling for my husband? The officer was so happy and so pleasant sounding, that I wasn't particularly panicky. It mustn't be bad news or he wouldn't be sounding so jovial.

He was inquiring if Randy had a Pontiac Grand Am, which he didn't. The nice officer didn't seem satisfied with this answer and continued to pepper me with questions: "He doesn't have a Pontiac Grand Am? Are you sure? How well do you know Randy?" Finally, he said, "Ma'am, I am *telling* you, Randy owns a Pontiac Grand Am." He sounded so happy!

And then it clicked — we had *won* a Pontiac Grand Am! Oh my God, it was unbelievable! There had been a huge hospital lottery happening locally with hundreds of prizes. We had been practicing the "law of attraction," by cutting out pictures of the prizes. We had been visualizing and now here it was; we had won a car! I am on my cell phone in an elevator and I am sooo excited!! "Oh my, God, we won a car! I can't believe it!" I keep repeating this into the receiver.

"Ma'am, ma'am, this is the Police Department, *we don't give away cars*," said the kind officer in a firm voice, trying to calm me down. What? Ohhhh. My party was pooped — no lottery, no prize, no car. It had all been a silly misunderstanding. I had forgotten that our son's Grand Am was insured under Randy's name. He had parked it overnight at my Mom's building and the police thought they were returning our stolen car to us.

Enlightening Strikes.

While, it would be fun to win, I suddenly realized that I had already won the lottery. By the sheer fact that you are reading this, I know that you too have won the lottery of life. If you are like me, you have so much food in your fridge and cupboards that you often don't know what to have for dinner. You could go out to pretty much any restaurant tonight if you so choose. You've been well educated and have had lots of opportunities. You have a circle of family and/or friends who love you. You have a roof over your head, a comfy couch to relax on and maybe even a good book in your hands.

Yep, you have won the lottery of life. Congratulations!

Now, what can we do to show our appreciation for winning the lottery of life? Here are some ideas:

Stop by your closest community police station and pick up some free graffiti wipes to use in your community. They are like smelly baby wipes that easily take graffiti off of buildings, fences, mail boxes, etc.

Take some extra bags on your next walk and instead of complaining about the litter, pick it up.

Spend a few hours at a local shelter, food bank or somewhere that you can lend your able body to help others.

123

Join in a charity event to support a cause you believe in — you will be active and raise money and awareness.

Visit elderly people and offer to shop for them or take them out for a treat.

Spend the first five minutes and the last five minutes of each day reflecting on your blessings.

We give and we get, lottery or no lottery — choose to be happy anyway.

FOCUS ON WHAT YOU ALREADY HAVE AND YOU WILL START TO SEE MORE OF THE GOOD THINGS IN YOUR LIFE.

Would This Be Considered a Miracle?

"We spend too much time worrying about how we will make things happen. Be open to the possibility that the world will conspire in our favor." Steph

Right then I knew I was about to witness a miracle. I sat and listened to what was transpiring with silent tears streaming down my cheeks.

She was a professionally trained singer, turned wife, mother, teacher and business owner. At the core of everything else she was and did, was her music. Julie's music was her passion, her escape, her outlet for expression; it was a part of her. It fit in some ways into her real life, but not in every way. In fact, lots of people who knew "this" Julie didn't know about her passion, and of those who did, many were not supportive.

"Are you still into that? Aren't you happy with your life?" The implication was that she should stop playing with the past.

Julie knew something they did not. She did not want to make music *instead* of her real life; she wanted to make music *within* her real life. Mini violins and other instruments took an important place in Julie's home and heart, and she would sometimes even share her music with her students.

Julie loved her life, but she wanted to record her songs, her way. She did not want to be a *star;* she wanted to record her music for her children and for others to enjoy, but mostly for herself.

With a busy family and career and all the things that go with it, the money to record a CD just wasn't at the top of the priority scale. Yet she knew that someday, although she did not know how, she *would* make this CD of original music.

Julie was my son's Grade 7 teacher and one day I saw her on her front lawn and went over to say hi. "I have just written a new song," she said after a few moments of chit-chat. "Would you have time to come in and hear it?" How could I say no to this request? Yet, part of me dreaded it. What if it was really bad? That would be so awkward! Nonetheless, into the house we went.

She played her guitar and sang her song and I was shocked. The song she sang was beautiful; she had a voice like an angel, and I was, quite literally, moved to tears. When she was done, she sat back and said, "I don't know why I invited you in to hear this. I have never done anything like that before." "People need to hear you," was all I could say.

Julie and I became fast friends and that summer she had the opportunity to play at a small festival. As her biggest fan, I agreed to make the two-hour trek to watch her debut. I decided it would be fun to bring the kids and make it an outing to see their old teacher.

The festival was in the evening and because Julie was the grand finale, it would mean we would be very late, too late to drive home. In a bold move, I asked a friend if the kids and I could sleep over at her cottage, which was close by, when the concert was over, and she graciously agreed.

The evening was beautiful; the crowd was excited and Julie was…petrified. You see, what I didn't know about Julie was that although she was a professionally trained vocalist, she had only recently taught herself to play guitar. This was to be her first public performance singing *and* playing and she had ice cold feet. My coaching was not working so well at this point, even though I was pulling out everything I knew. The anxiety overpowered the coaching.

When it was finally her turn, Julie tentatively got onto the stage; she looked so nervous, so unsure. I was petrified for her. Then she opened her mouth and the proverbial hush fell over the crowd; she was awesome and they were mesmerized by her voice.

Suddenly, everything went crazy. A drunk started being disruptive. Someone tried to silence him and the next thing we knew, equipment was flying all over the stage, and people were running and screaming. A campground brawl had begun and our party was clearly over.

When we were safely away from the mayhem, and over the shock, we were so mad. This bozo had ruined her opportunity to shine. All the work, the anticipation, the travel — all for one song. Ugh. Then I had a great idea, why not go back to my friend's cottage, maybe sit around the campfire, and have our own little private concert? Done deal.

As we were driving back, I suddenly panicked. I had just invited people to the cottage. The problem was…it was not *my* cottage! Oops. And it was not just Julie; she had her family in tow — three kids, her husband and in-laws. Oh my God, what did I do? My kids where chastising me the entire way, "Mom, you can't just invite people over to someone else's cabin!" They were right, but it was too late, I had already done it.

I sped ahead to get to the cottage in time to warn my hosts and apologize for what was about to happen. Fortunately, Sharon and Mark are the epitome of gracious hosts and they were incredibly understanding and wonderfully welcoming, and we all gathered around a bonfire for a lovely evening.

 When Julie finally brought out her guitar and began to sing, it was a very special moment. Our hosts talked to her about her musical aspirations and then I realized that this **Enlightening** had struck about a year ago, but today was the day it would unfold.

You see, Sharon and Mark were not just ordinary friends, they were especially blessed friends — especially blessed friends who were closet philanthropists. But I knew, and although words were never spoken, I had seen this moment coming in my mind. Unbeknownst to Julie, I had told my friends about her and had even given them a basement recording she had done. They were strangers to Julie, but she was not a stranger to them.

Right there, around the campfire, my friends gave Julie a $15,000 check to record her CD — no strings attached, no matching half and half, no receipts, no repayment schedule, no percentage of sales, *nothing*. They simply said, "It's your turn," went to the picnic table and wrote her a personal check for $15,000 — that's with three zeros!

I swear I couldn't have been happier if that check was in my name. To witness that experience was life changing for me.

I learned so incredibly much from the time I first heard Julie sing, to when I was at her CD release party. First, that we don't always need to know "how" things will happen or unfurl. We get consumed with the *how*, and when we can't figure it out, we just stop. Perhaps if we could just trust and believe a little bit more. If we could keep working our passion and our truth, the "how" of the situation would resolve itself. Often, life does have a wonderful way of working out.

Second, that sometimes you don't understand why things happen. Perhaps ours is not to question why, just to accept and move on to the next open door.

Third, that people are wonderful, period. You hear report after report of terrible things happening in the world, but this was so affirming that people *are* indeed wonderful. Ordinary people can make extraordinary things happen.

And lastly, that even when every fiber in your body is screaming, "No, I can't take this, do this, be this, or have this," you sometimes have to cross your fingers, take a big breath, and jump.

That year Julie produced two amazing "products," her fourth daughter and her debut CD.

What experience in your life seemed awful to you at the time, but turned into a blessing? If there is something challenging going on right now, try to flip it to see a possible upside.

BELIEVE IN HUMANKIND,
BELIEVE IN GOODWILL,
BELIEVE IN MIRACLES.

Don't Let the Grilled Cheese Win

"A person without a sense of humor is like a wagon without springs. It's jolted by every pebble in the road." Henry Ward Beecher

For my entire adult life I have been noted for my grilled cheese sandwiches. They are quite famous at my house, not because they are extra tasty, but because they are extra burnt. They are not just burnt sometimes; they are burnt *all* the time. They are burnt not because the stove cooks too hot or because my cookware is cheap, although I have used both of those excuses. They are burnt because I consistently do two things wrong. I leave the heat on high and then I leave the kitchen "just for a minute" to do something else. The result: one side golden, the other side black, every time.

You might think I would learn after a year or two, but apparently not. Grilled cheese, burnt on one side, is my specialty. What's yours?

One day, as Randy and I were preparing to go camping, he decided to make a grilled cheese sandwich. I was in the kitchen packing, but I glanced over and admired his technique for churning out the perfect sandwich, golden brown on both sides. My patient husband never burns his grilled cheese; he focuses on his task at hand, with the heat on low.

For some reason, on this day, things did not work out as planned. With the burner on high he quickly stepped outside to do something, got sidetracked, and the next thing you know … sniff, sniff, "What's that burning smell?"

Randy was ma-ad! Not only because he was hungry, but because he always tells me what I'm doing wrong with my grilled cheeses, and this time he'd done the very same thing.

Tsk, tsk. For some nasty reason I felt somewhat good about his burnt sandwich! Shame on me.

He tossed his sandwich in the garbage and began to bang, crash and grumble around while preparing for our trip.

After a few minutes, I asked casually, "So, are you going to be cranky for the next 24 hours? 'Cause if you are, I don't even want to go."

"No," he grumbled.

"Well," I asked, pushing the envelope just a bit, "how many hours *are* you going to be cranky for?"

He stomped out of the house with a load of supplies for the car.

I spontaneously shouted after him, *"Don't let the grilled cheese win!"*

He stopped in his tracks and turned around. We made eye contact, and then the ridiculousness of that statement made us both howl with laughter, lighten up and move past the troubles.

Enlightening can send something profound even in a situation like a burnt sandwich. "Don't let the grilled cheese win" is not, of course, about grilled cheese. It is about every cranky person, parking ticket, stubbed toe, bad review, traffic jam, missed bus or rainy picnic you have ever encountered. It represents that "something" that is not going right, that has the power to ruin your day, week, month or life, if you let it. But it is also something that you can choose to let go of, laugh at, learn from. Scientific research shows that smiles and laughter, even if artificially induced, stimulate pleasure centers in the brain. That's *awesome*! Perhaps I should walk around with a pencil in between my teeth so that I'm smiling all the time?

I used to get angry at silly things and be angry for a long time, too long. Now, when I recognize those nasty feelings starting to bubble up, I try to squash them immediately. Life is too short to be angry for too long; we need to learn to flip the switch, to lighten up and to let go. One of my favorite techniques for mood shifting is to look up to the sky, tilt my head and smile. It is physically impossible to be cranky in this position! Of course, music, meditation and visualization all can be used to shift your mood. Having an arsenal of tools that you know will work for you when you are in a bad mood can be a lifesaver.

Grilled cheese has taken on a whole new meaning in our house, and it never fails to make us chuckle. Whether it is ongoing little challenges, or major life shifting ones, always remember: Don't let the grilled cheese win!

Consider creating a list of mood shifters for yourself.

COLLECT AS MANY POSITIVE, MOOD SHIFTING IDEAS AS YOU CAN SO YOU WILL HAVE A STASH TO DRAW FROM WHEN YOU NEED THEM.

Oh, Paulo!

"We can rationalize things to death, but in our hearts, we know what the right answer is." Steph

I love Sudbury. Sudbury, Ontario. Sudbury, Ontario, Canada. While it may not be an exotic locale, Sudbury is the place dreams are made!

I was speaking in this sleepy Canadian town in February. Let me describe Sudbury in February: cold and dark, yep, that's about it. My engagement was over and I wasn't due to fly out until the next day. I was in a downtown hotel with nothing to do and time to kill. There was a gym attached to the hotel that we were allowed to use; so off I went.

I was excited to see a spin class happening shortly, so I hung around in the spin room waiting for it to start. In strode Paulo, a tall, dark and handsome fellow with a Spanish accent — yum. Paulo, it turned out, was the instructor and I was suddenly more eager than ever to go cycling through the Alps following his lead. We introduced ourselves and made small talk while we waited for some other participants, but strangely, no one else came.

Not wanting to be the only one in the class, I said, "I don't want you to teach this just for me. I'm fine doing something else in the gym instead."

133

"Oh, no, no, no," he said, in his beautiful, thick accent, tight bicycle shorts and skimpy muscle shirt, "we are going to do this together."

"Well, if you insist," I concede. Excuse me; I have a date to go cycling through the virtual Alps, with Paulo.

And so we rode. We rode our stationary bikes for an hour over hill and dale, fast and slow. We chatted and laughed and sweated, we burned our requisite amount of calories, and had about as much fun as you can when you are practically dying.

After the workout, out of the blue, Paulo blew my mind, "Would you like to go out for a drink?"

Out for a drink? Me? Out for a *drink*? Me? I look over my shoulder to see if he is talking to someone else. No one else is there. *Me*???

I'D LIKE TO GO FOR A DRINK, BUT MY *BODYGUARD* WON'T ALLOW IT.

Hold on here, I need to press the pause button. I have been married for a long time, a long, long time, and no one has asked me out for a drink in even longer than that. Maybe I have forgotten the cues, the lines, the way it goes? What does asking "out for a drink" mean nowadays anyway?

Enlightening is banging on my head, but I am not answering this time. Shut up, I tell it, leave me alone, I *want* to go out for a drink with him.

I am thinking, actually, I am rationalizing that this is part of my vision. I have actually written it down: To travel extensively and meet scads of interesting people. Well, I was traveling, and he was an interesting people. What would a little drink hurt?

Enlightening is persistent if nothing else. I know, I know, something here doesn't seem right. Does he mean a drink or *drink*? Does he mean coffee and chat or drink and...? I am totally up for a coffee and chat, but if it's a drink and something else, I don't want to send the wrong message. Or am I flattering myself? I am very confused in this nanosecond while he is waiting for an answer. Could this be one of those "crystal-clear yeses?"

"Oh, Paulo, *thank you* so much for asking, but I have to say no."

"Are you sure?" says the guy who should be the next Calvin Klein model.

135

No, I am not sure, I think, but I say, "Yes, but thank you."

This is, perhaps, the most sincere 'thank you' I have ever said. Thank you Paulo, you young, tanned, gorgeous, fit, Spanish cycling master. Thank you for making this older, married woman feel like a woman, even if you did just mean coffee and chat.

I skip all the way back to my hotel room and I am smiling from ear to ear. I want to tell everyone, *"Paulo asked me for a drink!"* I don't need to go, but thank you for asking Paulo; I love you for asking!

When temptation comes my way – whether it is something as complex as infidelity, or something as seemingly innocuous as gossip, I have three criteria to run through:

• Is this okay? If I have to ask, it's probably not.

• How would (insert name of someone I respect) handle this?

• Would I do this if my spouse/partner/parent/ child was watching?

The answer comes easily after that litmus test.

When I get back to my hotel room, Randy phones — my wonderful, loving, trusting husband who *never* phones me when I am on the road — to see how I am. I am so great I tell him, "Paulo asked me out!"

"Who's Paulo," he asks? It doesn't matter, what matters is I love you, and I am so happy that I married you and that you trust me, and that I trust me, and life is good, and I am still a woman, even if I am old and married and have a stack of kids and a bunch of bills at home. Did I mention that I love Sudbury?

WHEN YOU ARE THINKING OF TAKING THE LOW ROAD, ASK YOURSELF, "WOULD I DO THIS IF SOMEONE I RESPECTED WAS WATCHING?"

The $20,000 Breakfast

"Making the decision to have a child is momentous. It is to decide forever to have your heart go walking around outside your body." Elizabeth Stone

Gather 150 seventeen-year-old young men, dress them up in their finest attire, stuff them into a crowded auditorium to sit beside their mothers for three hours, and things are bound to get interesting.

After scrimping and saving and tweaking our budget, we had come up with the $5,000 a year tuition to send our son to a private school that we had hoped would help him get excited about his education and his future. Four years times $5,000 equals a big investment.

On the Friday before Mother's Day of his graduation year, we moms were treated to a morning of celebration. Although it was quite "hush, hush," we had heard whispers about it from other moms who had been there before us. We had some idea of what to expect, but still we were not prepared.

The morning began with a celebration service, with a rose and a tissue packet for each mom. Each boy — big strapping football players, small late bloomers, smart kids, challenging kids, quiet kids — all crossed the archway to manhood. Each had one minute with the microphone. One minute to look into his mother's eyes and tell her what was in his heart. One minute to condense his entire lifetime into words that would last forever. Just one minute to bare his soul in front of 300 others.

Some boys had been up all night searching for the perfect words, some had been working on this for months. All were stressed, nervous and more than a little petrified. We Moms felt their anxiety and it started to rub off on us.

Everyone took pity on the poor boy that had to go first. With sweaty palms and a quivering voice, he began and set the wheel in motion. One by one, each boy stood with his mother, introduced her by name and began. Many boys started with, "This is my beautiful Mom." For most of us that was enough to get those tissue packets open and set the waterworks flowing.

I listened intently to each boy.

"Mom, I didn't really want to go to this school, when all my friends where going to 'regular' school, but Mom I am so glad you made me come here. I will send my own son here too."

"Mom, I have worked for months on this speech and I can't stop crying long enough to read it to you."

"Mom, thank you for years and years of packing my lunches."

"Mom, thanks for *not* packing my lunches, for *not* doing everything for me so I can be a capable adult."

"Thank you Mom for the thousands of miles of driving you've done."

Others went on to thank their mothers for giving up the best piece of chicken and the biggest slice of cake. Some said they were sorry for late nights and missed curfews, for not being respectful or for the bedrooms and bathrooms left in various states of disrepair. Some dug out wrinkled papers from their suit pockets; some just spoke from the heart. Some sang a song written especially for the day. Others crooned the songs their mother's had sung to them as a child. One young man started to sing "You are my sunshine" but couldn't get through it; still he wouldn't let go of the microphone or his Mom until he choked out every last word.

It was absolutely gut-wrenching to watch. I felt privy to the most intimate moment a mother and son could share. Some boys read prose; some wrote their own poetry expressly written for this day; some recited quotes and some just cried and barely uttered a word.

How could it be that each moment seemed frozen in time, yet went by in such a blur? Each boy's speech was unique and beautiful, poignant and sincere; each one perfect. Never had I heard the word "mommy" used by so many grown boys, unapologetically, unabashed, uninhibited, even surrounded by all their peers. Some draped over their mom's shoulders as they choked out the words that had been buried for so long, an "I love you" that hadn't been said and hugs too infrequently shared. Each boy-man who spoke was raw, honest and

140

genuine, and each mother listening must have felt their hearts either skip a beat or stop beating altogether. The moms spoke no words that morning. Mouthing "I love you" was about the most we could muster. Besides, this was not our day to speak; it was our day to listen, just listen.

When it was Aaron's turn to stand he said: "Mom, we exchange I love you and hugs and stuff all the time, but I want to say in front of everybody how much I love you. You have always been there for me and always believed in me, and always encouraged me not to settle for less than I deserved or am capable of. You are my rock, Mom."

A hug is the only thing that can possibly follow.

Enlightening struck in an unusual way that morning in May. I thought that day was about me and my son and I was wrong. It was not just what *my* son was saying to *me* that was important. These boys were speaking to mothers everywhere, on behalf of children everywhere. They were speaking for the children who could not find the words or the courage or the right time or the right place. They were speaking for those who wanted to forgive, who wanted to say "I'm sorry," who wanted to move their relationships forward, who wanted to start fresh, who wanted to tell their mom that she was their mentor, their guide. It was a thank you given for things that can never, ever be repaid by children who understood; children who finally "got it."

141

The sacrifices that we made as parents — financial, emotional and social — were unequivocally answered on this beautiful day in May. After 150 "one minutes" were up, everyone gathered in the schoolyard to pray together and plant a tree in honor of the growth and personal development these young men had experienced.

The event is over, words have been forgotten, new memories and milestones are being achieved, but the depth of feelings, the emotional and spiritual connections of that day will be remembered forever.

On those days when you think your kids just don't get it and you wonder if they ever will; on those days when you question every decision you have ever made and are not sure everything you gave up was worth it, please let this story remind you that you are doing the right thing. They *will* get it and it's worth the wait!

The $20,000 breakfast — a bargain in my books.

P.S. This story was first published in *Chicken Soup for the Soul*. I bet you have an inspiring story that is itching to be published! Think about it, then write it, then submit it – you just never know.

Surprises (revisited)

"A fellow who does things that count, doesn't usually stop to count them." Albert Einstein

"I would like an orchid for my birthday," I tell Randy. "They are at the grocery store and are about $25. I've always wanted an orchid."

Life is easier now that I just ask for what I would like, no expectations, no disappointments. It's just a simpler way to live, after all, I can't read his mind either.

In he trods on my birthday with the requisite orchid, proud and happy he has accomplished his mission. I look at the orchid and laugh. This is, without a doubt, the *ugliest* orchid I have ever seen. I didn't even know they made ugly orchids. Forgive me, but it looked like a scrotum. Yes, it did. And so it was renamed the scrotum plant, and we got at least $25 worth of laughs from its presence. I made a secret plan to kill it as quickly as possible.

"Did *you* think that was a nice plant?" I question.

"No, but that's what you asked for, so that's what I got," Randy replies, sensibly.

The next day he comes home and declares, "I picked up something else for your birthday, it's in the garage."

"Great," I say unenthusiastically, "a new orchid?"

143

I open the garage door. I see a car. A brand new car. A brand new car with "Happy Birthday" balloons on the roof.

I wouldn't even believe it except that the kids are snapping pictures and everyone is wearing huge smiles.

"You bought me a $%^@# car?!"

Audible gasps are heard. This is the first time my kids have ever heard me say that word. I couldn't help it; that's what came out.

I think I might die of shock. After 20 years of no surprises, he buys me a car? Are you kidding me?

"Why did you buy me a car?" I barely squeak out.

"You deserve it," he says sincerely.

Enlightening encases me in a hug, and at that moment I know it is not about the car at all. It is about all the care, thought and love that went into picking out this beautiful, perfect surprise many months ago. Some people asked, wouldn't you have liked to pick out your own car; chosen the color, the style? Absolutely not, this car is perfect. I feel like I am wrapped up in love every time I get in it.

They say you can't change people, but I'm not so sure, because the more kind and patient and loving I am, the more kind and patient and loving people are to me. The more I have evolved and grown, the more other people seem to have evolved and grown along side of me. Maybe it's osmosis, or

144

possibly diffusion, I don't know. Remember, I wasn't that good in school. Whatever it is, I like it!

If you want to be a leader, you go *first*; if you want people to be friendlier, you go *first*. If you want more surprises, you go *first*. Whatever it is you want more of, you go *first*.

WHATEVER IT IS YOU WANT
MORE OF, YOU GO FIRST.

Sing Me a Song, Piano Man

"If you don't like something, change it. If you can't change it, change your attitude." Maya Angelou

The vast cold airport is full of people but a lonely place, nonetheless. This is a part of speaking for a living, lots of travel. Usually, I like it; sometimes it's tough.

People are buzzing around focused on their destinations. Bags are lugged and rolled; fast food is gobbled with coffee to go. It's not too exciting to be waiting for another plane. But hold on, what's that? I hear music. I follow the music to find a baby grand piano with a young man at the keys. The music flows effortlessly from his fingertips and I take it all in. There is one stool nearby, and I ask if I can sit down. He looks shocked, like he is not asked that question often. He has many CDs for sale; clearly he is an accomplished musician.

What I really want to do is close my eyes, block out the airport surroundings and get lost in his music for awhile; but instead, we end up chatting for a bit. I learn that he plays at the airport everyday from nine to five, stopping only for short breaks. People pass by and rarely clap, although he says he really appreciates it when they do.

"What's this like for you," I wonder. "Is it hard?"

"No," he says, "I love playing music; it's my passion." There's that word again. Passion.

146

It can help you override a lot.

After a spell, I realize that now I must hurry to catch my flight. I am pushing it a little close. I purchase a CD with pleasure.

The Minneapolis airport is so long that I decide to run over to catch the tram. It will surely get me to my gate quicker than walking the quarter mile. I am wrong. The tram goes exactly 10 feet and dies. We are stuck; minutes pass like hours. The thought of *Fantasy Island's* Tattoo yelling, "De plane, de plane!" runs through my head. I consult with the other prisoners in the tram and ask permission to press the emergency button; they agree. A calm voice comes over the PA system: "Don't panic, you are safe, a technician will be around soon."

"Not soon enough," I think.

Tic, tic, tic, finally we see the technician sauntering towards us. Shouldn't he be running? He calmly lets us out and we balance beam on the ledge back to the terminal. And then I run! I run down the moving walkways. I run past all the people and parcels (clearly I have worn the wrong shoes for this). I run a quarter mile to the last terminal. It is not populated; this is not a good sign. I throw my ticket on the counter, optimistic I have made it just before the plane door is closed and the flight to Kentucky has left.

What? The plane *has* left? Left? *Left*? Noooooo!

147

I look out the window in case the attendant is wrong. She's not; there is no plane in sight.

But I was stuck on a tram! It wasn't my fault! I start to play the blame game. It was the piano player that delayed me, the tram, the tram repair guy that walked sooo slow. On and on I go. It's funny how whenever I look for someone to blame, I always find at least one person. Then I do what any (female) motivational speaker would do; I cry. The attendant wants to help me, but I am not ready. Enlightening wants to help me, but I ask them both to please wait a wee bit; I am busy with my own personal pity party. I have never missed a plane before. I need a moment. I give myself five minutes to squawk, grumble and whine, to no one in particular.

When the time is up, I invite **Enlightening**, my old friend, back. I reframe, regroup, breathe and move forward willingly. I ask myself my famous, million-dollar question: "What is my role in this?" I slowly move from the unhelpful, "Why me?" to the pro-active "How can I make the situation better?"

It wasn't the tram that made me late; I was already pushing the envelope when I got on the tram. If I would have given myself a reasonable amount of time, the 15-minute delay (it only felt like hours) on the tram wouldn't have mattered. It was my own fault. I know there is a reason that I was not meant to be on this plane, but the "why" doesn't matter. Perspective shifted; attitude lifted.

They would have to reroute me via Memphis to get me to my speaking engagement on time. Well, I've never been to Memphis; does it count when you are only in the airport? During the flight, I ask my seatmate what he would recommend to pass an hour in the Memphis airport? "Bar-B-Que!" he says, practically salivating. "You *gotta* have the Bar-B-Que — pulled pork on a bun. It's famous 'round these parts!"

Excellent, I thought, that's what I will do.

As soon as you enter the terminal in Memphis, you can smell it! Now, *I* am salivating. I purchase the sandwich, and it's *yum*! I decide missing your plane is not the worst thing in the world. I guess I was meant to have lunch in Memphis.

While I love playing board games, the blame game is a lost cause every time.

Next time you are tempted to play the very disempowering blame game, consider asking yourself this very empowering question, "What is my role in this situation?" I bet it will lead you to winning the game of life.

IF YOU PLAY THE BLAME GAME,
YOU WILL LOSE EVERY TIME.
INSTEAD ASK YOURSELF,
"WHAT IS MY ROLE IN THIS?"

A Vision of Beauty

"That which is striking and beautiful is not always good, but that which is good is always beautiful." Ninon de L'Enclos

It was Kara's turn to celebrate her graduation. Like the other 103 girls from her school, she was dressed to perfection — the makeup, the nails, the hair — all arranged just so. And then there was the dress — wow! Champagne in color, strapless, with a lightly beaded bodice, it fit her like a glove, right off the rack. I was so proud of her; she was a beautiful young woman out enjoying her special night.

Twenty-four hours later, we had flown over two countries, and were in the war-torn nation of El Salvador on a two week humanitarian trip.

Two years prior, as a family project, we had each made a vision board — a collage of what we wanted our future to look like. This messy but fun project is an annual tradition in our family, usually happening around New Year's Day. Sometime we make them into posters; sometimes we make them into placemats. Either way we always learn something about ourselves and each other.

That year, Kara's board included a picture of a dark-skinned child, and when I asked her what this image signified, she said it represented the mission work she wanted to do someday. Inspired, I made a promise to her that if she went, I would go too. Truthfully, I didn't think she would really go because you have to get immunized, and she is petrified of needles. But her desire to go overrode her fear of needles, and the next thing I knew we were both packing for El Salvador.

The thing was that she wanted to go, and I did not.

I was not happy about how much money this "trip" was going to cost, and I was not happy about how much work I would be missing. All I could think about was what I was giving up in order to go away. But a promise is a promise, and poof, there we were in the remote village of Loma Linda, Central America.

Then I saw her, a dishevelled, grubby girl drenched in sweat, with braids in her hair and a sweatband around her head. She had the most gigantic smile on her face; she had children dripping off of her, just like the sweat was. They couldn't get enough of her; they were touching her and patting her; she was lifting them into the air and swinging them around; they were putting fresh picked flowers into her hair. Despite the language barrier, their communication was flawless — it was the universal language called love.

My daughter was a mess, and I had never seen her look more beautiful. In fact, all the other young women in our group were exactly the same — a sweaty mess, and so gorgeous it made me cry.

I asked myself, what is more beautiful – young women dressed to the nines, primped and polished and perfect; or young women connecting countries and building a bridge of love between cultures? The answer was crystal clear.

This **Enlightening** took all my worries away. I scolded myself for my selfishness, for not wanting to spend my time and my money. Shame on me. These people had what we would perceive as "nothing." The very least I could do was to give up some time and resources to make a tiny difference, to have some understanding of what they go through. The trip proved to be an emotional, spiritual, educational, physical and cultural experience that inspired changes in all of us who made the journey. I learned to see beauty everywhere, even in the poverty; there were so many beautiful people and moments. I learned that it is not about building *the* bridge as we assumed; they had enough people to do that kind of work. Instead, it is about building *a* bridge between our community and theirs. It's about letting them know that other people care about them and their situation. It's about what we do with the information once we go back to our "real" lives. It's about how we can accomplish positive change and influence ourselves and others.

Although we started the trip as mother and daughter, it was soon evident that my role there was not as a mother. I was there as an equal to my daughter; both of us were learning and stretching and growing simultaneously. As often happens when we set out to try to do something for someone else, we get so much more in return.

I decided that once I was home, I could continue to help my new friends in Loma Linda. I decided to buy jewellery from local artisans to sell at the back of the room when I was speaking. The money would help purchase bus tickets, uniforms and supplies for students who couldn't afford these basics. It was a win-win for all!

I never would have had this beautiful experience if it weren't for the gentle but persistent nudging of my daughter, and I can't help but wonder if she would have discovered it without her vision board.

What did you see that was beautiful today?

TRAIN YOUR MIND TO
SEE BEAUTY EVERYWHERE.

Juggling in the Airport

"Judging others does not make them so; it just makes you judgmental." Author unknown

Isabel doubled over in laughter. "If I saw someone doing that, I would think they were a nut!"

"Oh," I said, sobered by the thought that she was probably right.

Sometimes I get a brilliant idea; the problem is that sometimes no one else thinks it's brilliant, except me!

I knew I would have many, many, many hours to kill during a double stopover flight and there is only so much reading one can do. So, I decided that I would teach myself to juggle in the airport. Yes, you read that right, and I know that might sound a little odd. The funny thing is, at the time, I didn't think this was strange at all until I mentioned it to my client.

Suddenly, her laughter had me second-guessing my decision; I *would* look like a fool. That's too bad, I thought, because I have always wanted to learn to juggle, and I imagine it takes a lot of time to learn and when else would I have down time like that?

 Knock, knock. Who's there? **Enlightening.** Good buddy, what do you think about this dilemma?

Well, you've always wanted to learn to juggle, right? Yes.

And this is a good time to learn, right? Yes.

And you care what complete strangers think about you? Yes.

Why? I don't know exactly.

Are you hurting anyone? No.

Then do what you want to do.

I trust Enlightening now; everything good has started with enlightening.

Okay, I will learn to juggle in the airport, if only to prove Isabel wrong! I am armed with three hacky sack type balls and three lines of translated instructions. Do this; do that; do the other thing; repeat. How hard can it be? *Very* hard.

It is *very* difficult to learn to juggle, and *very* good exercise, too. My quads are killing me from all of the bending down and picking up! But, so far, the great things about it are far outweighing the bad. I meet every little kid in each airport, each one attracted to my bright, colorful juggling balls; their parents seem grateful for this distraction and the kids and I have great fun together.

Then I meet a doctor who is determined to teach me how to juggle. "I juggled as a child," he brags.

Apparently he is not a child anymore, because he cannot juggle now. He is very upset that the technique is not coming back to him.

"I'll get it again, just give me a minute," he says, focused on his task.

To repeat, the *doctor* is juggling in the airport, or trying to at least. He will not give me back my balls until our flight is called.

"I hope you don't need a doctor while you're away, but just in case," he says, handing me his business card.

Over the years, there have been so many things I have not done, said or been because I was consumed by what I imagined other people would think about me. People who don't love me, people who don't know me, people who I don't even like — why would I care what *those* people think about me? No more. From now on I will run things through my own filter and/or the filter of people who I love and who care about me. That will be my guiding light.

What have you given up or not started because you were worried what other people would think? I hate to tell you, but people don't care all that much about what you are doing; they are too busy worrying about what other people are thinking about what *they* are doing! They may *notice* what you do, but then they go on with their day. If they want to talk, let them talk. As long as you are not hurting anybody, go on, just do it!

I come home and proudly juggle for Isabel. She is suitably impressed.

"I have a gift for you," she beams. "I saw this in the store and I thought of you right away." The gift is a yo-yo. She saw a yo-yo and thought of me. Funny, Isabel, very funny!

ONE OF THE BIGGEST OBSTACLES THAT PREVENTS US FROM ACHIEVING UNCOMMON SUCCESS IS THAT WE CARE TOO MUCH ABOUT WHAT OTHER PEOPLE THINK.

The Mourning Ritual

"Sometimes you get an answer in a way you never thought you would, to a question you never knew you had." Steph

When I say I have a great idea, my family usually says "oh-oh" and runs the other way. My clients on the other hand are very trusting!

This particular fall day an email announcement came by my desk. It was announcing an event called "Wailing." With it was a brief message that described the evening as "creating a sacred space to touch and explore our grief, anger and sense of loss and giving you a way to honor and express these feelings." Now, while I was not particularly sad or angry at the time, I thought of Cathy, who had some unresolved issues. On a whim, I phoned her up and told her about this very unusual event which was happening that very night.

Much to my surprise, she said, "Sure, I'll try anything, if you will come."

Half an hour later we were driving out of town to a remote little area with scarcely a house in sight. When we saw the locale we were both a little apprehensive. It was quite deserted and we didn't see many other cars around. Nonetheless, we ponied up and went inside. The woman in charge sensed our discomfort (or was it so blatant that she saw it?) "This ritual is historical and sacred in many cultures," she said. "Don't

159

worry, I will facilitate everything. You have no need to be anxious."

"Okay," we said, hopeful but unsure.

Nothing, except perhaps a YouTube video, could have prepared us for what we were about to experience.

Try to imagine being brought out into the night to a small garage with a half dozen other women. Inside, it is dark except for a fire pot burning on a small table in the middle of the room. There are dry, dead leaves strewn all over the floor around the firepot with a circle of chairs around the outside of the ring of leaves. There are sounds coming from a portable sound system; it is not really music, though; it's a recording of lonesome wolves howling, aw-wooooooo. We are instructed to walk around the firepot, stamping our feet and crushing the leaves.

We weren't sure what to do. We looked at each other, certain that we both wanted to run away, but we were there and we didn't want to hurt anyone's feelings. So we walked and we stomped. Just when you thought it couldn't get any stranger, the facilitator gave us each a bunch of dead branches for us to wave around. Seriously? We walked around the circle with the other women. We stomped; we waved our branches. Just when we thought it *really* couldn't get any stranger, we were instructed to howl along with the "music." Cathy and I exchanged glances again, and then we reluctantly continued to walk around the circle — stomping, waving and howling. Just as we thought it *surely* can't get any stranger, she pulled out a collection of black veils and explained a brief history of the veil and how it was used to give women the privacy they needed to conduct this mourning ritual. Everyone got a veil. We were now walking about in the circle, stomping, waving, and howling in the dark garage under the cloak of our black veils. Yes, this really did happen; who could make up something like this?

Personally, I was very thankful for the veil, I experienced emotions that I didn't want other people to see. Part of me was panicking about how Cathy was handling this, and whether she would kill me or not for bringing her here, and the other part of me was (very disrespectfully, I might add) laughing, which was clearly inappropriate. I understand that rituals such as these are sacred in some cultures, but I just couldn't believe that we were actually doing this! I pictured someone peeking in and thinking that there was some sort of cult-like activity going on here.

Just when we thought it *absolutely* couldn't get any stranger, our patient facilitator pointed out a part of the garage we had yet to notice. There was a corner of the building that was blocked off by cardboard and beside that there were a lot of random pieces of china. No, we were not sitting down to break bread together; we were going to break china together. Seriously? Was this for real?

"As the urge arises," she said, "grab a piece of china and smash it on the floor. Do this as much and as often as you like. There are thick, permanent markers over here so you can write words on your dishes; you can smash them or keep them," she instructed.

I wanted to go home; this was too much for me. Again, I was torn. This seemed very wasteful of perfectly good china. If my mother could see what we were doing, she would not be happy. Yet, I could tell this wailing thing was working for some of the women. They were really getting into it and you could feel the anger, sadness, grief palpably in the garage. It was not a happy place to be.

Still, I was not that sad or angry, and mostly what I felt was just ridiculous. But when in Rome … We walked around the circle. We stomped, waved and howled under our veils, and eventually I picked up a piece of china and threw it very unenthusiastically on the hard concrete garage floor. It shattered into thousands of tiny shards. I picked up the marker and more china, and I wrote words like hate, anger, envy, and jealousy on my dishes, and I broke them one at a time - each smash giving me permission to add more oomph to my throw. I wrote on and smashed more china. Have you ever broken dishes on purpose? It is a very weird feeling. I kept thinking my Mom was going to come in and give me heck!

After a bit, I found it actually felt good. I was beginning to see the benefit of this. Then something happened that really surprised me. I found myself getting emotional. The combination of sounds of wailing women and breaking dishes was upsetting, and memories of things I was upset about started welling up. Issues I thought were long gone crept back. I was becoming a stomping, waving, howling, smashing wailer!

Enlightening is back. It tells me, NOW. Now, is the time to finally and sincerely, forgive my grandmother, my parents, and mostly myself. We all did the best we could with what we had and what we knew at the time. All of that happened to bring me to this point in my life, and I *love* this point in my life. All that history made me who I am. Our family *not* getting help cemented the fact that I don't want anyone else to feel that there is no one to turn to, no one to help them, no other answers. I am a helper; it is who I was born to be and that's not so bad after all. I do deserve to be happy.

I took a piece of china and wrote, "Just Love Anyway" on it. In that moment, that was my answer to a question I didn't know I had. It felt good; it felt right.

For the last piece of the wailing puzzle, we were given paper and a pen and the opportunity to write down whatever we wanted, and then to throw it in the fire. Literally and symbolically letting it go. I find it fascinating that I don't remember what I wrote — like it really *is* gone.

After the paper burning, the whole group went into the house and had dainties. It was kind of like we were at a funeral, except we paid $20 and everyone was still breathing.

As we got into the car, finally away from everyone else, Cathy looked at me and said, "Please tell me we never have to do that again."

I shook my head, "No, no we don't."

At the end of the day, while I won't likely be wailing again anytime soon, I may look at garage sale china with new eyes. What if you flattened an old cardboard box and left it in your garage with some old, chipped china? What if when you were red with anger, you could go out into the privacy of your garage, open up your box, smash 'til your little heart was content, have the mess nicely contained and then carry on with your day? It would most certainly beat yelling at the kids, insulting your spouse or putting a dent in the wall. We all need a healthy way to deal with our "issues," whether it's journaling it out, punching a pillow or getting professional help.

At the end of our evening, I came home with my "souvenir" veil and my "Just Love Anyway" plate. As I was telling my family, "You won't believe what happened tonight…" and just then, without warning, the plate jumped out of my hand and smashed onto the floor into thousands of tiny shards. Go figure!

YOUR NEXT GREAT ADVENTURE
IN LIFE IS WAITING TO BE
UNCOVERED. GO FIND IT!

Things I Will Never Do

"The miracle is not that I finished, it's that I started." George Sheenan

Every June, sixteen unique women with sixteen different ideas about life, gather at a special cottage.

No topics are off limits. You may have heard jokes about what men talk about when they are together, but nothing surprises me more than what women will divulge in a safe setting. Chatter about kids, husbands, careers, sex, challenges, triumphs, dreams, fears. The goal is not to solve anyone's problems, the fun is in getting to know each other and ourselves better.

This year, one interesting question was posed: "Name something you will *never* do."

The answers are a great mix of funny, strange, expected and surprising.

What would you answer?

I think hard, at this point; there is not much I won't try. "I will never go in a triathlon," I finally state firmly.

"You know," says Shelley, the fit one, "at my lake, they have this thing called a Try-a-Tri. It's a mini swim, bike and run. They have it every August." In an instant I can feel that familiar shift; it's enlightening again, and already I know that whatever this try-a-tri thing is, I will be doing it.

I went from a "never" to an, "Oh, really, that sounds interesting," in about three seconds.

The only problem is that I cannot swim; in fact, I cannot even put my head under water without plugging my nose. It's very embarrassing to be a grown woman and have to plug your nose to go underwater. Perhaps this is the push I need to overcome my fear of water.

Somehow, despite the fact that I cannot swim, I have given birth to mermaids, and so it is that I have two live-in swim instructors who can teach me. One is slow and gentle, "Come on Mom, you can do it." The other is strict and serious, "Get over it and just put your head under, already."

What a joy to learn to swim, be able to submerge my head and throw my nose plugs away! Along with my training buddy, Marie, we work hard to prepare for the event. We swim and bike, then bike and run, then run and swim. We are *ready*!

Oh no, we are not ready for this! The temperature has plummeted. It is cold, raining and windy. It never once crossed my mind that it wouldn't be perfect outside, that the lake wouldn't look like a pool, or that I would be petrified.

The lake actually looks foreboding and dangerous. The swim is the first event of the three. I am so scared. I can feel the tears welling up behind my eyes; I will them to stop. They do not listen. They come pouring out. I don't know what a panic attack is like, but I imagine it is pretty close to this. Poor Marie is out of her element too; she does not know what to do with me. *I* don't know what to do with me. I am a mess. "I want to go home; I don't want to do this anymore; I changed my mind," I cry. Shelley, who is there to cheer us on, ensures that she gets this embarrassing display on video for posterity. Thanks Shelley.

Marie says, "Where is the other Stephanie, the 'motivational speaker' Stephanie? I don't know what to do with this one. Bring the other one back."

I cannot; the "other Stephanie" is gone. This one can barely swim and is so scared of the treacherous looking water.

Just in the nick of time, **Enlightening** strikes — thank God. Face the fear and do it anyway; face the fear and do it anyway; face the fear and do it anyway; I repeat. My fear: I am petrified of the water. Reality: I can swim. Reality: it's not deep. Reality: there are boats to pull me in if I get tired. Reality: it will be cold, but I will not drown.

Plunge — into the water we go. I hate to say it's not that awful, but it's really not that awful. Too bad I used up so much of my energy panicking. We swim, we bike, we run — well it's more of a slow jog — nonetheless we complete the triathlon and live to tell the tale. At the end, even with the anxiety attack, I am proud of myself. It feels so good to have met that fear and to have beaten it down.

After the event, there is lots and lots of food and even a chocolate fondue. If they would have just told me there would be chocolate in the first place, I probably would have been just fine.

I encourage my clients to set big goals, like my tri was for me. Having a big "why" can be the "carrot in front of your nose" to lead you to do things you never thought you would do.

Gather a supportive team; face the fear and start from where you are, with what you have.

P.S. I am not sure, but strictly for your amusement, I *might* post the anxiety attack video on the site... maybe!

STOP WAITING FOR A BETTER TIME, BETTER CIRCUMSTANCE, BETTER ANYTHING. THE BETTER TIME, THE PERFECT TIME, IS RIGHT NOW.

The Fugitive

"If you want to be happy, be." Leo Tolstoy

This seems wrong on so many levels; I am mad, bad and sad all at the same time.

"I'll take my bike and meet you at the golf course," I told Randy. I was proud of myself for picking fitness over convenience, and off I went to meet our friends for a round of golf on a lovely holiday Monday morning.

But I was soon to be in for a big surprise!

The sound of a police cruiser and the flash of the lights catch my attention. Funny, no cars are around. No way, they couldn't possibly be stopping *me?* On my bicycle?

Yes, they were! I stopped my bike and the cop ambled over.

"Ma'am, you went through a stop sign on a residential street."

"Yes," I admitted, "I did."

"Name please," he asked.

They entered all my info into their computer and started writing. "You're not writing me a ticket, are you?" I could feel the tears welling up in the back of my eyes. I bit my lip, trying to hold them back.

"Yes, I'm sorry, we are." In fact, it was to be a $199.80 ticket *plus* a demerit on my driver's licence, I was informed. I tried to rationalize, sweet talk and beg my way out of the ticket.

Wait, let me rewind and try that again; I'll stop twice, I promise!

Too little, too late, the fine is mine and I am left literally crying on the side of the road. I lean against a tree in shock, disgust, anger.

I figure riding my bike while crying is at least as dangerous as riding through a stop sign – maybe more so. I pick a tree by the side of the road, sit down and weep into my hands. I can't help it; I am sobbing. I am having another pity party; leave me alone.

But nooooo …

A stranger has been lurking, watching this incident unfold. He has walked back and forth, with his dog, around our scene numerous times. He comes over to my tree and bends down. He is madder than a hatter (not sure what that means exactly – but he is angry!) He can't believe the cops would do this; he is swearing up and down; his language and rage frighten me. He calls the cops every name under the sun. Is this supposed to make me feel better?

His rant has made my thinking shift – you see my son is trying to get onto the police force. My protective mother instinct flares up, and I hear myself talking this guy down.

They are just doing their job.
I did go through the stop sign.
It was my fault.
They don't like giving tickets.
They don't assign the penalty.
They are not bad people, they have to do this.

On and on I go, until he walks away in disgust.

I imagine someone talking to my son, a future officer of the law, this way - having people hate him when they don't even know him. I start crying all over again.

The next thing I know, another fellow pulls up.

He pulls over and asks, "Stephanie, are you okay?

Great, he knew my name, and here I was looking like someone who needs to go to a psych ward for evaluation. Without looking up, I figured it was probably Dave.

I was happy, grateful and relieved to see Rob, a Toastmasters colleague. He let me talk and cry by my tree. He listened, he commiserated with me, but did not swear or advise or condemn. He gave me just the right mix of sympathy and encouragement. He was a friend, just when I need one.

I regain control of my emotions and pedal home. Randy gives me a long hug instead of a long lecture, which is greatly appreciated. I have lectured myself enough already.

I am not happy with my ticket. A warning and $50 fine would have left the message with me but, you know, **Enlightening** can be costly. I'd screwed up and the police had just been doing their job. They hadn't had fun doing it, but they'd done it. If we want them to be there for us when we need them, in times of emergency, danger, crisis, then I guess we have to understand that they are also around when we would rather they not be, like when we disobey the law. Maybe they saved my life, who knows? People are surprised that I am not enraged about this ticket, but it makes me happier to think of it this way. I am sure Anthony would be proud of me, too and, after all, when I am 92, how important will this be? Taking a bird's eye view of upsetting situations is a quick way of de-escalating. Whether it is a ticket or one of life's other annoyances, choosing a perspective that will lend itself to understanding, less drama and ultimately increased happiness, is my pain control of choice.

So, suck it up princess, pay your ticket and stop at stop signs, even on your bike. And do me a favor, give your local police force the respect it deserves; you couldn't pay me enough money to do that job.

HOW IMPORTANT WILL
THIS ISSUE BE IN FIVE DAYS,
FIVE MONTHS, FIVE YEARS?
HOW LONG CAN YOU
WAIT TO BE HAPPY?

P.S. Almost one year later, I was scheduled to appeal this ticket in court. The moment I stepped into the court room, I was told the charges had been dropped. People asked how I 'beat the system' – I told them I just showed up. Isn't that half the battle in life, too? Just show up.

The Right Wrong Number

"How wonderful it is that nobody need wait a single moment before starting to improve the world." Anne Frank

I couldn't help it. My daughter told me not to; Randy told me not to; but I did it anyway. I called the wrong number back, on purpose.

But it wasn't just any wrong number, it was Anthony.

I had tried to call a client a few days prior and discovered I had dialed a wrong number.

"Sorry to bother you," I said to the elderly gent on the other end of the line.

"Oh dear, it's no bother, in fact, this is the highlight of my day. I am 92 and I'm just sitting on my porch and I haven't talked to anyone all day. It's so nice to hear your voice!"

Zap (**Enlightening** responds quickly)

Stephanie, are you going to make a difference or just hang up? I want to make a difference, but I am running late and I have a hundred things to do. It's not a good time to chat on the phone with a stranger, I reason, but luckily I don't listen to myself.

I asked him his name and told him mine and we talked about life and love like we were old friends. His voice was so delightful that I not only could I feel his spirit and energy right through the telephone wires, I could feel mine being lifted as

176

well. Our delightful conversation absolutely and totally made my day.

For weeks, in fact, I talked about this stranger, I told everyone I knew about Anthony and then, well, ignoring my daughter's claim that I was "stalking" him, I decided to call him back.

"Hi, Anthony, this is Stephanie."

"Who?" Oh no, maybe my daughter was right?

"The wrong number that called you a while back."

"Oh, dear, how wonderful to hear your voice again!" he beamed. Whew!

We had another wonderful conversation. And then it just popped out of my mouth, "Anthony, do you listen to the radio?"

"Yes, I am mostly blind, so I listen a lot."

"What station do you listen to?"

"CJOB." Bingo!

"Anthony, listen tomorrow around four and I am going to say hi to you on the air, okay?

He thought this would be great fun and planned to tell all his family about "us." I used Anthony's story as my motivational moment on the radio. The listeners loved the story.

And then, I couldn't help it, I called him *again*. This time I asked him if I could speak to him live on the air. He was so *thrilled*, sooo excited! He called everyone he knew and told them to listen in.

And when I called him on the air, he was a *rock star*! His story is amazing, he taught himself how to read after he retired, he speaks many languages (seven I think it was), and he was a war hero. He had to cut off the foot of a man who was stuck under a burning truck, which exploded just after he got them both to safety.

On the air, I complimented his constant cheery disposition and asked him how he kept his positive frame of mind. At 92, how did he handle it when things went wrong or people treated him badly? How did he remain so happy?

"People are great, my life has been great, the world is great and that's that," he declared.

"Okay, Anthony, but what do you do when people annoy you, disappoint you, hurt you? How do you handle that?" I questioned.

"Never happens."

"Come on now, you are 92 and no one has ever annoyed you?" I persisted. Now I am wondering if he has a little dementia.

"Nope. People are wonderful," he maintained.

Even though he nursed the love of his life through terminally ill cancer at home, even though he literally woke up blind and deaf one morning, even though he has war stories that would make you cry, his attitude outshines everything else.

His mindset is only on the positive and I know that I want to be like him when I grow up. This man is living and breathing uncommon success!

After the show, his granddaughter wrote me a letter and verified everything. She wrote, "He's learned everything he could, taught himself what he needed to know, *always* treated others with the same respect and dignity, and his general outlook on life is as a journey, not a destination. All my life, that man has been exactly the same and when he told you he's never had anything annoying happen to him, it's just because he doesn't let things bother him too much or for long. I honestly don't know how he does it, because there has been enough just cause for him to be soured over the years."

When the show was over, I knew I needed to meet this amazing gentleman in person. With his granddaughter there (just to ensure I wasn't too crazy) I was able to meet Anthony in person. We visited for over an hour and before I left I asked him if I could videotape a short interview with him. With the camera rolling, I asked him how he kept his upbeat attitude, despite tough times. I will never forget what happened next. Anthony slowly looked up and pointed his crooked finger towards the window, "Everyday is a beautiful day," he said slowly and purposefully. "I don't care if it's raining or cold or what else is happening, *everyday* is a beautiful day." I got goose bumps. At that moment I knew I was privileged to witness something extraordinarily special. I knew that Anthony had given me the secret of life that day: "Every day is a beautiful day." Period.

Could it really be that simple? In this crazy, complex world, we continue to look for solutions that are equally complex. Perhaps the answer is as simple and perfect as Anthony's answer. "Every day is a beautiful day." And that's that.

You don't need to start a foundation, travel to Third World countries or speak to thousands of people to make a difference. You just need to seize opportunities, as simple as a wrong number, recognize the potential to make a small shift and act on it. Every day we have the opportunity to make a difference, to let someone else shine. As it is usually, I felt like I gave a quarter, received a twenty and was thanked for the transaction.

Why wait for great, big, momentous events to occur? Peek under every rock, around each corner and take the chances, big or little, as they come. And whether things work out or not, know that every day *is* a beautiful day.

Thanks Anthony for shining your light into my world.

YOU DON'T HAVE TO START A FOUNDATION, TRAVEL TO A THIRD WORLD COUNTRY OR GIVE UP A KIDNEY TO MAKE A DIFFERENCE. JUST LOOK FOR OPPORTUNITIES—EVERYWHERE!

Epilogue

The book is done, but the journey is not. I can't wait to see what happens next for both of us. It is my sincere hope that within my stories you have found your own; that although our struggles have been different, the similarities have stood out. I hope that the ideas shared within these pages have helped you hear what you needed to hear and will help you do what you need to do.

I hope that *Enlightening* will strike you many times as you navigate the twists and turns of your life. It is in these moments that we can choose to step up, step down or step out. We can choose to take it or leave it, to see the obstacles or the opportunities, to change or to stay the same, to go or to grow. I hope the next time something significant (or seemingly trivial) happens in your world, that your mindset will be stronger, and you will pull your own *Enlightening Strikes* moment out and let it help you create the mindset for uncommon success in your life.

As for me, this is where my stories end, for now. I do expect *Enlightening* to strike me many more times, as I have much to learn. Perhaps this is the end of the beginning.

And so I conclude, just as I began …

My name is Stephanie Staples and I don't care what the experts tell me to call myself. I am proud to be a motivational speaker. I am even more proud to be a common woman who has slowly discovered the secrets to creating a mindset for uncommon success. I feel happy, fulfilled, satisfied, and at the end of the day, that is what matters most, because that is when I can give my *best* to the world.

When the crowd goes home and the evaluations are filed away, I am left with one lingering thought from an audience member. It is perhaps the one that lights me up the most. She wrote … "Wow, you really live your life."

Yes. Yes I do.

Now it's your turn to live Your Life, Unlimited!

About the Author

Stephanie Staples makes her home on the beautiful Canadian Prairies with her awesome family; Randy, Aaron, Kara, Gina and a menagerie of pets. She thinks you already know too much about her, but if you really want to know more, there are 30 things you *don't* need to know about Stephanie on her website, visit => http://www.YourLifeUnlimited.ca .

Invitations for you:

To coach with Stephanie ...

Find out more information about how her coaching services can benefit you please visit =>

http://www.YourLifeUnlimited.ca/coaching/html

To contact Stephanie ...

To share your questions, challenges, wins or feedback, drop a line to Stephanie@YourLifeUnlimited.ca

To receive Stephanie's complimentary resources...

Start getting to know yourself better today, with the *Your Life, Unlimited Guided E-Journal.*

Sign up to be a part of this positive, pro-active Your Life, Unlimited community and receive a monthly *Motivational Moment* in your in-box. To receive these life-enhancing tools visit => http://www.YourLifeUnlimited.ca

Keynotes, Retreats and Seminars with Stephanie ...

When your company, group or association is ready for a little inspiration, perspective shifting and, of course, *motivation*, then inquire about Stephanie's speaking or coaching services by stopping over at => http://www.YourLifeUnlimited.ca.

To socialize with Stephanie ...

Get short bursts of motivation to lift your spirits, fun videos for kicking life up a notch and lots of interaction with Steph and our Facebook community full of like-minded, upbeat people => http://www.facebook.com/YourLifeUnlimited

Follow her on Twitter, too => @stephanestaples

For information on special sales or bulk purchases for this book call: 1-204-255-5912

Thank You

To my husband; Randy you are the love of my life. I simply couldn't do any of "this" without you. Thank you for allowing me to be and to grow and for supporting me, always.

To my favorite children; Aaron, Kara and Gina, thank you for making me stretch, holding me accountable and teaching me everything I need to know. It has been a privilege to parent all of you. You've done great; I am one proud Mamma!

To my Mom; Lillian Scarnati, who, at 87, continues to inspire me with her ongoing commitment to personal growth. Thank you Mom for all you are to me and the world.

To my Dad; Albert Scarnati, whose bravery started my ball rolling.

To my clients and colleagues; thank you for trusting and believing in me and my work, for helping me help others, and for your ongoing guidance along the way.

To Lea Brovedani and Michelle Cederberg, my wonderful 'master-minders' and to my volunteer readers, who plugged through this manuscript, gave critical suggestions, helpful feedback and listened to all my insecurities associated with pouring out my heart and soul for the world to see. Thank you so, so much.

To Susan Sweeney, coach extraordinaire, without you this book would still be in my head, not in your hands. I will never forget when you phoned me from Barcelona – that's when I knew I could really do this. You have an amazing gift, thank you, thank you, thank you for sharing your time and expertise with me.

To John Hindle, thank you for using your TLC to make the second coming of W.E.S better than the first.

And finally, to you the reader; for believing in uncommon success! Thank you for growing yourself stronger and making our world a better place.

Steph xoxox

Made in the USA
Monee, IL
05 November 2021